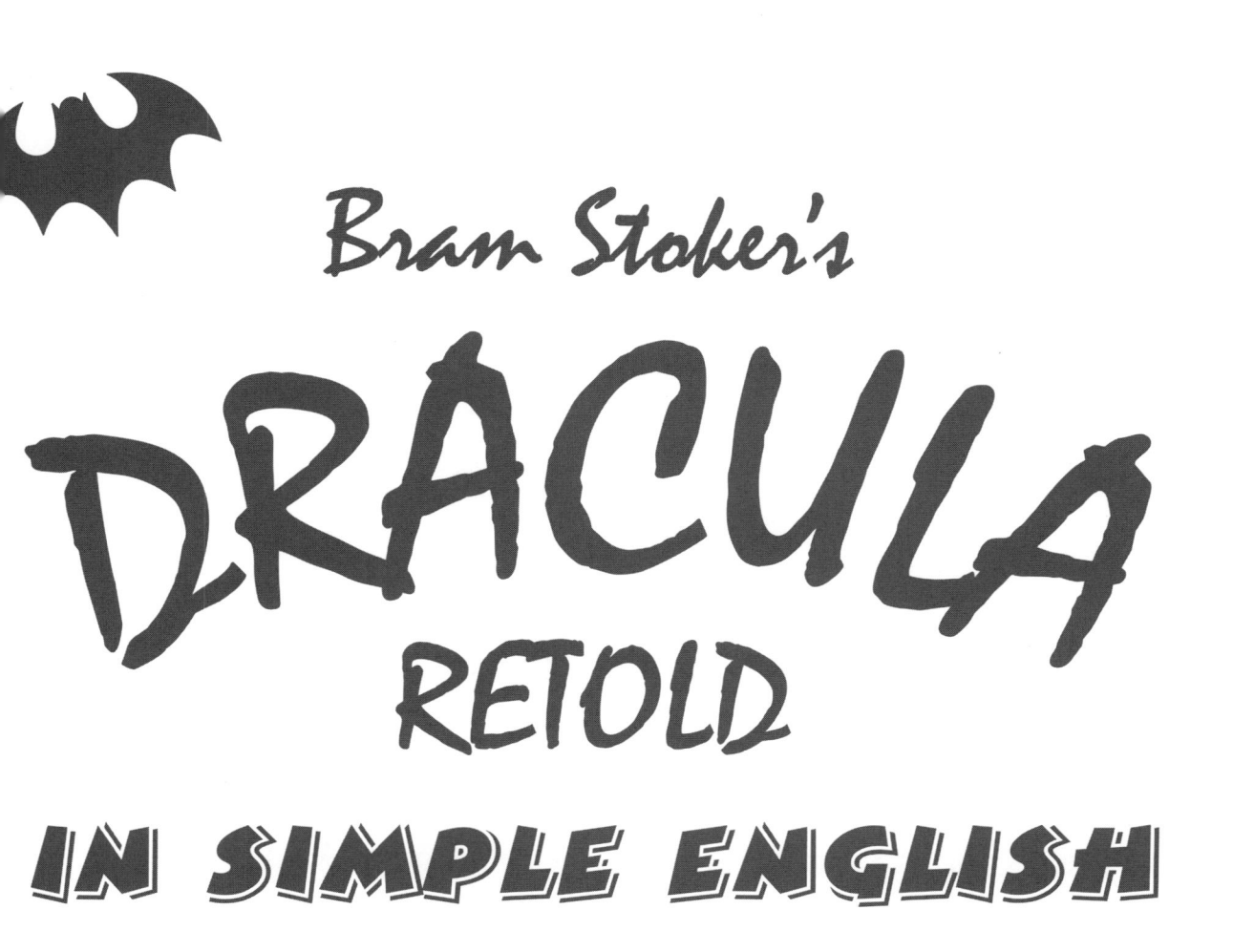

Bram Stoker's
DRACULA
RETOLD
IN SIMPLE ENGLISH

Arranged by Yuko Hosokawa

JN222984

EIHŌSHA

音声ファイルのダウンロード方法

英宝社ホームページ（http://www.eihosha.co.jp/）の
「テキスト音声ダウンロード」バナーをクリックすると、
音声ファイルダウンロードページにアクセスできます。

Contents

Chapter 1　ハーカー、トランシルヴァニアへ ————5
　　　　　　To the Borgo Pass ／ The dead travel fast

Chapter 2　ドラキュラ城に囚われて————11
　　　　　　A prisoner of the Castle ／ A sweet dream made of horror

コラム1　『ドラキュラ』の作者ブラム・ストーカー ————17

Chapter 3　伯爵の出立————19
　　　　　　In the vault ／ The Count leaves

Chapter 4　死者たちの船————25
　　　　　　Lucy and her suitors ／ Renfield and his geometric progression of life
　　　　　　The Count arrives in England

Chapter 5　ルーシー、「侵入口」となる————31
　　　　　　On the East Cliff ／ The first transfusion

コラム2　『ドラキュラ』—執筆のきっかけとモデル————38

Chapter 6　ルーシー、「戦場」となる————40
　　　　　　The Professor researches ／ The Count's last visit

Chapter 7　不死者ルーシー ————47
　　　　　　Lucy passes away ／ Lucy, the undead

Chapter 8　ヴァン・ヘルシングの分析と戦略————54
　　　　　　Setting Lucy free ／ Working out a strategy

Chapter 9　ミナの危機————60
　　　　　　The confession of Renfield ／ Mina in a peril

コラム3　「血まみれの尼僧」から「女吸血鬼たち」、そして「ドラキュラ」へ————66

Chapter10　ミナ、「探知機」となる————70
　　　　　　Cornering the Count ／ Mina, the detector

Chapter11　再び、トランシルヴァニアへ————76
　　　　　　To Transylvania ／ To the Castle

Chapter12　終焉————82
　　　　　　The last battle ／ The end

コラム4　映画『ドラキュラ』————89

Appendix　　Chapter Introductions through Listening ————92

使用した図版について————97

～　学習者の皆さんへ　～

　予習をして授業に臨むことで「読む楽しみ」が増します。Get ready! で、語彙の準備や、必要なら土地名のリサーチをして舞台となる地理を把握し、Enjoy the story! の「予習のための質問」の参照となる英文の部分を特定し、日本語で答えをまとめておきましょう。なじみのない地名については「19 世紀＋地名」「世紀末＋都市名、地区名」など、検索を工夫して、画像やストリートヴューでイメージを掴んでおきましょう。

　授業は、皆さんの復習と予習を確認するクイズ、あるいは Appendix のリスニング英文完成練習で始まるかもしれません。Listening in and acting out! では、パートナーとアイコンタクトをとりながら声に出して練習してみましょう。授業後は、登場人物の行動やストーリー展開を復習し、新しく出会った語彙や表現を書き出して自分だけの「ドラキュラ・ノート」を作ってみましょう。印象や文脈に支えられた効率的な学習方法です。

～　主な登場人物　～

ドラキュラ伯爵　Count Dracula　トランシルヴァニアの城に住む。ロンドンに不動産を購入しようとしている。

ジョン・セワード　John Seward　ロンドンに精神病院を持つ医師。

ヴァン・ヘルシング教授　Professor Van Helsing　オランダ、アムステルダム大学の医学博士。奇病に詳しい。セワード医師の師にあたる。Dr Van Helsing とも the Professor とも言及される。

ジョナサン・ハーカー　Jonathan Harker　ロンドンの事務弁護士。ドラキュラ城に出張する。

ミナ・マレー　Mina Murray　ジョナサンの婚約者。結婚してミナ・ハーカーに。

ルーシー・ウェステンラ　Lucy Westenra　ミナの友人。アーサー・ホルムウッドと婚約している。

アーサー・ホルムウッド　Arthur Holmwood　スコットランドの貴族。

クィンシー・モリス　Quincy Morris　アメリカ人富豪。アーサーの友達。

レンフィールド　Renfield　セワードの病院の入院患者。命を取り込むことに取りつかれている。

Chapter 1

ハーカー、トランシルヴァニアへ

👤 *Get ready!*

授業に臨む準備をしましょう。

Ⅰ 日本語と英語を一致させてください。

1 邪悪な　　2 十字架　　3 ギラギラ輝く　　4 にやりと笑う　　5 特徴のある
6 購入　　7 不動産　　8 風変りな　　9 吐き気　　10 抑える

peculiar　nausea　suppress　purchase　property
distinctive　evil　crucifix　sneer　glitter

Ⅱ Google Map で次の場所を確認しておきましょう。

Bistritz in Hungary

1 Munich in Germany
2 Bistritz now in Hungary
3 Transylvania, Bukovina, and the Borgo Pass, now in Rumania
4 The Carpathians

⚰ *Enjoy the story!*

予習のための質問です。答えの参照となる英文部分を特定し、答えを日本語で準備しておきましょう。

1 What brought the solicitor named Jonathan Harker to Transylvania?
ジョナサン・ハーカーという事務弁護士がトランシルヴァニアに来た理由は何か。

2 What did a passenger on the coach suggest by "The dead travel fast"?
馬車の乗客は、「死者は速く移動する」という言葉で何を示唆したのか。

3 What made Jonathan Harker think that he had had a dream while riding in the Count's coach?
ジョナサン・ハーカーは、なぜ伯爵の馬車に乗っているあいだに夢を見たと思ったのか。

4 What did Count Dracula say to Jonathan Harker in welcoming him at the entrance of his castle?
ドラキュラ伯爵は城の玄関で何と言ってジョナサン・ハーカーを歓迎したか。

5 What did Count Dracula look like as Jonathan Harker observed him?
ジョナサン・ハーカーが観察したドラキュラ伯爵の外見はどのようなものか。

To the Borgo Pass

Solicitor, Jonathan Harker's diary written in Bistritz

May 3rd

On the first of May, I left Munich for Transylvania. On the way, I was welcomed by a very friendly landlady at the Golden Krone Hotel here in Bistritz. She asked me, "The English gentleman? Going to the Castle of Dracula in Transylvania?" When I said "Yes", she handed me this letter.

Dear Friend,

Welcome to the Carpathians. Sleep well tonight. Catch the coach for Bukovina at three tomorrow. My coach will be waiting for you at the Borgo Pass.

Your friend,
Count Dracula

Dracula, 1931, Lugosi / Tod Browning Version

May 4th

A little while ago, the landlady came up to me.

"Do you have to go, young gentleman? Do you know what day it is today? It's the eve of Saint George's Day."

She then continued, "All the evil things will have complete power at midnight tonight." I didn't understand what she meant, and I think it showed on my face. She fell on her knees and begged me not to go. When I said that I had to go because I was on a business trip, she took a crucifix from her neck and put it on mine, saying "Take it for your mother's sake." I felt a bit worried without knowing why. Here comes the coach!

May 5th

I am at the Castle of Dracula now.

When I got on the coach yesterday, some people listened to the landlady and then came around me. They repeated some words in Slovak and Serbian. I looked up those words in my multilingual dictionary and found their meanings — "werewolf" and "vampire". They crossed themselves while seeing my coach off.

It seemed that the driver wanted to arrive at the Borgo Pass as quickly as possible. Soon we saw the Carpathian Mountains above the hills on both sides of the road. As it became darker, the other passengers urged the driver to go faster. Then the mountains seemed nearer on each side. We arrived at the Borgo Pass and the coach stopped to wait for the Count's coach for a minute. But then the driver said to me, "You see, there is no coach waiting for you. Why don't you go to Bukovina for tonight and come back a few days later?"

As soon as he said this, the horses became excited and the passengers screamed and crossed themselves. Then a coach with four beautiful horses came along. Its driver was a tall man with a long beard. His eyes were glittering in the lamplight.

The dead travel fast

He said to our driver, "You are early tonight. I heard you telling the English gentleman to go to Bukovina." I wondered how he had heard the driver saying it. One of the passengers whispered, "The dead travel fast." The tall driver sneered. I could see his very red lips and sharp ivory teeth. He said, "Give me the gentleman's luggage." He put my luggage on his coach, and then reached me and helped me to get in. His handgrip was surprisingly strong.

We drove into the Borgo Pass. The coach went extremely fast. Somehow, I felt we were simply moving in a big circle going nowhere. So, I took a note of some distinctive rocks and trees. I'm sure I saw them several times. I looked at my pocket watch. It was almost midnight.

I then saw some blue flames by the coach. The driver jumped off towards it. Then, I think I fell asleep and had a

dream, for I remember a strange scene: the driver was standing between the flames and the coach but I could still see the flames through the driver. Another time, the coach was surrounded by a pack of wolves. The driver gave some command to them waving his arms. Then the wolves disappeared.

The journey seemed endless. But suddenly, I found myself in the courtyard of a half-ruined castle. The driver helped me out, jumped back on the coach, and disappeared. I was wondering, "Is this a usual kind of happening that a solicitor from London should experience when he is sent into a far foreign country to explain the purchase of a London property?"

Then I heard the large front door open with a heavy dismal sound.

Inside, stood a tall man with a long white moustache. "Count Dracula?" I asked. "Welcome to my house! Enter freely of your own will!" His English was excellent but of a strange intonation. He stood inside like a statue. But the moment I entered the castle he jumped closer to me and shook my hand. "Come freely, go safely! Leave something of the happiness you bring!" he said. The strength of the handshake reminded me of the driver.

He himself showed me to my room and invited me to dinner. I changed and went down to eat. The Count appeared again but said, "Eat as you please. But please excuse me, I do not join you, as I have already eaten."

After dinner, smoking a cigar, I observed his face. His large eyebrows almost met over the nose, which had peculiar nostrils. His lips were incredibly red, and

his teeth were sharp. His pale ears were pointed at the tops. The nails were long and fine. Strangely, there were hairs in the centre of his palms. Most annoyingly his breath stank. I felt a nausea, which I suppressed.

I　1～3と a)～c) を組み合わせて 3 つの文を完成しなさい。

1 The landlady of the hotel

2 The coach for Bukovina met the coach from the castle at the Borgo Pass

3 Count Dracula did not eat with Jonathan

a) because, if we believe the Count, he had already eaten.

b) gave her crucifix to Jonathan.

c) though the former had arrived there earlier than usual.

II　話の筋に沿って a)～e) を並べ替えなさい。

a) Jonathan had a strange experience while riding in the Count's coach.

b) Count Dracula welcomed Jonathan from the inside of the castle.

c) Jonathan received a letter of direction from Count Dracula.

d) The passengers of the coach for Bukovina wanted to pass the meeting point on Borgo Pass as quickly as possible.

e) The landlady begged Jonathan not to go to the castle.

🧛 **Tips for reading**

文修飾副詞

Strangely, there were hairs in the centres of his palms. (奇妙なことに～。)

(=It was strange that there were hairs in the centres of his palms.)

Most annoyingly his breath stank. （とても嫌だったのは～。）

(=It was most annoying that his breath stank.)

通常の副詞の例　His handgrip was surprisingly strong. (～驚くほど強かった。)

■英文を完成しましょう。

[　　　　　　] the plan worked. （幸運にも計画はうまくいった。）

=It was [　　　　　　] that the plan worked.

感覚動詞の第 5 文型

I heard the large front door open. （大きな玄関扉が開くのが聞こえた。）

The Count somehow could hear the driver saying it.

（伯爵にはなぜか御者がそう言っているのが聞こえた。）

■語句を並びかえて日本語に合う英文にしましょう。

1) ["vampires" in Slovak / some people / I / talk about / heard].

（人々がスロヴァキア語で吸血鬼のことを話すのが聞こえた。）

2) [between / I / the driver / standing / could see / the coach and the flame].

（御者が馬車と炎の間に立っているのが見えた。）

英語を聞いて会話を完成し、パートナーと口頭練習をしましょう。

A: Are you the English gentleman going to the castle?

B: Yes, I'm Jonathan Harker, [1   ].

A: Here's a letter for you from the castle.

B: Oh, thank you.

A: Sir, ah…. Do you know [2   ]? Do you have to go there tonight?

B: Yes, I must go there tonight. It is part of the business arrangement.

A: Then [3   ].

B: Your crucifix?

A: Yes, [4   ], please.

原作にチャレンジ (1)

Within, stood a tall old man, clean-shaven save for a long white moustache, and clad in black from head to foot, without a single speck of colour about him anywhere. He held in his hand an antique silver lamp, in which the flame burned without chimney or globe of any kind, throwing long, quivering shadows as it flickered in the draught of the open door. The old man motioned me in with his right hand with a courtly gesture, saying in excellent English, but with a strange intonation.

"Welcome to my house! Enter freely and of your own will!" He made no motion of stepping to meet me, but stood like a statue, as though his gesture of welcome had fixed him into stone. The instant, however, that I had stepped over the threshold, he moved impulsively forward, and holding out his hand grasped mine with a strength which made me wince, an effect which was not lessened by the fact that it seemed as cold as ice—more like the hand of a dead than a living man. Again, he said: "Welcome to my house. Come freely. Go safely; and leave something of the happiness you bring!" The strength of the handshake was so much akin to that which I had noticed in the driver, whose face I had not seen, that for a moment I doubted if it were not the same person to whom I was speaking; so, to make sure, I said interrogatively: "Count Dracula?

Chapter 2

ドラキュラ城に囚われて

👤 *Get ready!*

授業に臨む準備をしましょう。

I 日本語と英語を一致させてください。

1 貴族　2 侵略する　3 書類　4（鏡の）像　5 拒否
6 保証する　7 トカゲ　8 逆らう　9 感覚　10 半ば窒息した

invade　refusal　guarantee　lizard　disobey　noble
sensation　half-suffocated　documents　reflection

II 次の語句を辞書で調べましょう。

mansion　lunatic asylum　heathen　rage　vanity
precipice　protest　anticipation　furious

⚰️ *Enjoy the story!*

予習のための質問です。答えの参照となる英文部分を特定し、答えを日本語で準備しておきましょう。

1 What did Count Dracula seem to be concerned about regarding his stay in London?
　ドラキュラ伯爵は、ロンドン滞在の何を気にかけているようであるか。

2 What were the blue flames, according to the Count?
　ドラキュラ伯爵によれば、青い炎は何なのか。

3 Why did Jonathan Harker jump up when the Count saluted him?
　伯爵が挨拶をするとジョナサン・ハーカーが飛び上がったのはなぜか。

4 What horrified Jonathan Harker while he was watching the sunset scenery?
　ジョナサン・ハーカーは、夕日の光景を見ているとき何にぞっとしたか。

5 What happened when the blond woman was about to bite Jonathan Harker?
　金髪の女がジョナサン・ハーカーに噛みつこうとしたとき何がおこったか。

A prisoner of the Castle 🎧(1-4)

Jonathan Harker's diary

May 7th

In the morning before dawn, I found a kind of library. Some of the shelves were filled with books about England. Soon the Count came in and greeted me. "I learned your language through these books. I hope you can teach me how to speak it better."

"But you speak English very well," I said.

"I am a noble here. But in London, I will be a stranger. I will be nobody there." He seemed concerned about how he would be treated in London. In fact, he sounded worried.

"May I come to the library when I want to?"

"Certainly. You may go anywhere you wish in this castle, except where the doors are locked. We are in Transylvania. Transylvania is not England."

This led to my question about the blue flame I had seen on the way. The Count explained, "Our country, the land of Transylvania has been invaded many times by foreigners and heathens. So those blue flames appear to guard the buried treasure from the invaders once a year." Then the Count and I looked

at the documents I had prepared regarding his purchase of a London property, a large old house called Carfax. "Recently, one of the houses near this mansion has become a lunatic asylum," I reported to him. He signed the documents.

May 8th

I am glad to have written this diary. I need facts so that my imagination does not get out of control.

This morning, before dawn, I was shaving in front of my hanging mirror by the window. I heard the voice of the Count right behind me, saying "Good morning." I jumped up because I had not seen any reflection of his figure in my little travel mirror. Then I noticed a cut on my cheek in the mirror. It was bleeding. At the very moment, I sensed that the Count had come closer to me.

But I still could not see his reflection. I turned and looked at him. Then his face showed a rage and he tried to grab me by the throat. I pulled back and his hand touched the crucifix around my neck, which made an instant change in him. The rage had disappeared. He said, "Take care. Do not cut yourself. It may be more dangerous here than you think." Then he grabbed my mirror and said, "This toy of man's vanity has caused this trouble." And he threw it away from the window.

Later I went down, but I didn't see the Count. I went to the south window and found that the castle was located on a precipice— a precipice of a few hundred metres high! And doors, doors, and doors, all closed and locked. The castle is a prison and I am a prisoner!

A sweet dream made of horror

May 12th

I need to write down facts, just facts.

Today, the Count asked me if I had written my first letter to Mr. Peter Hawkins, my employer. I replied, "Yes, I have it here with me." He said, "Then write now to him that you will stay here for another month." I was about to open my month to protest but he said, "I desire it much. I do not accept your refusal." I saw that I was completely in his power. He added, "Please write only about business. Nothing else." When I finished writing, he took both of my letters, leaving me with this advice; "If you leave your room, never fall asleep in the other parts of this castle. I cannot guarantee your safety."

I was worried and needed some air. So later, I went up the stone stairs to the spot where I could look out of the window. It revived the feeling of freedom in me.

Watching the sunset scenery, I noticed something was moving. It was a man slowly coming out of the window below. The man began to crawl down the castle wall with his face down like a lizard. It was the

Count! To add to my horror, he was wearing my clothes.

May 16th
  Now it is early in the morning. I need to think about what happened last night. Was it a dream?
  Last evening, I saw the Count crawling down the wall again. I decided to explore some other rooms while he was out. I found a large door open ajar, so I pushed it and entered the room. It was a spacious one. Some old ragged pieces of laces and perfume bottles were scattered on the floor. The room must have been used by noble ladies a long time ago.
  Later I returned there because I took pleasure in disobeying the Count. I lay down on a couch looking out of the window. Then, I think, I fell asleep, for I am not sure if what I experienced was real or not.
  The room was the same, but I saw three young women. They did not make shadows in the clear moonlight. They came close to me and looked at me for some time. Two of them had dark hair and almost red eyes. The other one had blonde hair and eyes of sapphire. All of them showed brilliant teeth like pearls. They whispered to each other and laughed a metallic laugh. One of the women with black hair sat by me and said to the blonde, "Go on. He is young and there are kisses for all of us."
  I was lying with my eyes half-closed, with rather delightful anticipation. The blonde woman bent over me. Her breath was sweet but smelt like blood.
  Just when she was about to bite me, I felt some horrible sensation; I was aware of the presence of the Count in the room. He threw the blonde woman back and signalled the other two to leave the room. He shouted with a furious voice. "Do not touch him. He belongs to me."
  The blonde woman said to him laughing, "You never loved, you never loved." She asked, "Is not there anything for us tonight?" The Count threw a bag on the floor. She opened it. I heard a sound of a half-suffocated child. Then, I think, I fainted.

I 1〜3と a)〜c) を組み合わせて 3 つの文を完成しなさい。

1 While having a shave in front of his mirror, Jonathan noticed that

2 The Count crawled down the castle wall like a lizard

3 Jonathan felt delightful anticipation

    a) although the castle was on the precipice of a few hundred metres high.

    b) there was no reflection of the Count in it.

    c) when the blonde woman was about to bite him.

II 話の筋に沿って a)〜e) を並べ替えなさい。

a) The Count told Jonathan not to enter any of the locked rooms.

b) The Count signed the documents for the purchase of the property called Carfax in London.

c) The three women appeared to Jonathan when he was lying on the couch in a large room.

d) The Count tried to grab Jonathan by the throat when he saw a bleeding cut on his cheek.

e) Jonathan realized that he was a prisoner in the Castle of Dracula.

Tips for reading

名詞節を含む文

1) Dracula was worried, "How will I be treated in London?"

Dracula was worried about *how he would be treated in London.*

（彼は自分がロンドンでどう扱われるかを心配していた。）

2) The Count asked me, "Have you written your first letter?"

The Count asked me *if I had written my first letter.*

    （伯爵は私に、最初の手紙を書いたのかを尋ねた。）

■もとの英文と同じ意味になるよう、あとの英文を完成しましょう。

1) I asked myself, "Was what I experienced real?"

I asked myself if [   ]

2) "What day is it today? Do you know?"

Do you know [   ]?

3) She asked, "Is not there anything for us tonight?"

She asked [   ] that night.

「, 」に続いて前の語句や節を先行詞とする関係代名詞 which

I pulled back and his hand touched the crucifix around my neck, *which* made an instant change in him.
（身を引くと十字架に彼の手が触れ、そのせいで瞬間的に彼のようすが変わった。）

■次の英文を完成しましょう。

He said, "Transylvania is not England," [   ] to my question about the blue flame.
（彼は「トランシルヴァニアはイングランドではないのだよ」と言い、そのことが青い炎についての私の質問につながった。／そこで私は青い炎について尋ねた。）

▌Ⅱ▐ *Listening in and acting out!*

英語を聞いて会話を完成し、パートナーと口頭練習をしましょう。

A: Where is the letter I requested you to write?
B: [1   ].
A: Then write one more letter telling that you stay here for another month.
B: For another month? [2   ]?
A: Yes. And I will not [3   ]. I also warn you, I can't [4   ] if you sleep in the other parts of the castle.

原作にチャレンジ (2)

But at that instant another sensation swept through me as quick as lightning. I was conscious of the presence of the Count, and of his being as if lapped in a storm of fury. As my eyes opened involuntarily I saw his strong hand grasp the slender neck of the fair woman and with giant's power draw it back, the blue eyes transformed with fury, the white teeth champing with rage, and the fair cheeks blazing red with passion. But the Count! Never did I imagine such wrath and fury, even in the demons of the pit. His eyes were positively blazing. The red light in them was lurid, as if the flames of hell-fire blazed behind them. His face was deathly pale, and the lines of it were hard like drawn wires; the thick eyebrows that met over the nose now seemed like a heaving bar of white-hot metal.

コラム1 『ドラキュラ』の作者ブラム・ストーカー

　ブラム・ストーカー（Abraham "Bram" Stoker, 1847–1912）は、イギリスから独立する前のアイルランドの出身である。生前は『ドラキュラ』の作者というより、むしろ俳優で演出家であるヘンリー・アーヴィング (1838-1905)の秘書として知られていた。アーヴィングは、ロンドンの、今は『ライオン・キング』のホームとして知られるライシアム劇場（Lyceum Theatre）のオーナーでもあり、ストーカーは劇場マネージャーも兼任し公私にわたって彼を支えた。

アーヴィング

　ストーカーは、7才まで一日のほとんどをベッドで過ごすような病弱な少年だった。しかし作家としての資質を育んだ、とふりかえり、幼年期についてこう述べている。

I was naturally thoughtful, and the leisure of long illness gave opportunity for many thoughts which were fruitful according to their kind in later years. (*Irish Times*, 23 April 1912) （生まれつき物思う性質で、長い病いの怠惰な時間は後にそれぞれ実のりとなる多くのことを考える機会を与えてくれた。）

ロンドン、ライシアム劇場

　長じてはダブリンのトリニティ・カレッジに進み、アイルランド人恐怖小説家シェリダン・レ・ファニュが主宰するダブリン・イブニング・メール紙（*Dublin Evening Mail*）の演劇批評を担当した。そのときロンドン王立劇場で上演されたアーヴィング主演の『ハムレット』を賞賛する記事を書き、それがきっかけで二人は親しくなったとされる。

　その後ストーカーはダブリンで公務員として働くようになり、かたわら小説やドキュメンタリーを発表していたが、1878 年、女優フロレンス・バルコムとの結婚を機にロンドンに移った。フロレンスは美しさで知られた奔放な女性で、世紀末を代表する作家オスカー・ワイルドにも求婚されていた。おそらくワイルドとストーカーはフロレンスを通じて知り合った。余談であるが、のちにワイルドが「男色」の罪による刑を終えてロンドンの人間関係から逃げるようにフランスに移ったとき、ストーカーは失意の底にあった彼を友人として訪ね、励ましている。

ワイルド

　ロンドンに移ったストーカーは先述のごとくアーヴィングの秘書兼マネージャーとなり、彼の過酷な要求をこなしながら、注意深い劇場運営とヒット作の連発によって、1878 年から 1905 年の間に約 200 万ポンドの収益を劇場にもたらした。

その間、1890 年から 1897 年まではロンドンのデイリー・テレグラフ紙 (*The Daily Telegraph*) の文芸記事も担当。そして 1897 年、『ドラキュラ』を発表。狙い通りその舞台も大ヒットさせたのである。

　彼は作品中、ドラキュラのホイットビー上陸を伝えるメディアとしてデイリー・テレグラフを実名で使っている。また、『シャーロック・ホームズ』シリーズの作者コナン・ドイルや画家の J・A・M ホイッスラーら、才能ある人々と親交を結んで刺激を受けた。ドイルからは「謎解き」の要素を学び、

ストーカー

また本書第 5 章の白衣の女性図はホイッスラーの作品であるがルーシーのイメージに重なる。さらにストーカーはアーヴィングに随行し世界のあちこち興行の旅をしたが、アメリカ滞在中ホワイトハウスに 2 度招かれたことがアメリカ人富豪モリスというキャラクターの採用に繋がったという。

　1905 年にアーヴィングが没すると、翌年、この当代随一の演劇人を身近に見て綴った回顧録を出した。これは今も「誠実正確かつ心を打つ」と高い評価を受けている。

　ストーカー自身は 1912 年 4 月 20 日、自宅で静かに息をひきとった。死因は何度か見舞われていた心臓発作とも梅毒だったとも言われている。

参考文献　*Something in the Blood: the Untold Story of Bram Stoker* (David J. Skal, Liveright Publisher, 2017)

Chapter 3

伯爵の出立

👤 *Get ready!*

授業に臨む準備をしましょう。

I 日本語と英語を一致させてください。

　1 地下納骨堂　　2 それぞれ　　3 強奪する　　4 誘拐する
　5 吠え声　　6 舌なめずりする　　7 おぞましい　　8 催眠をかける
　9 シャベル　　10 ぞっとすること

　mesmerise　　shudder　　howling　　lick　　dreadful
　vault　　shovel　　respectively　　snatch　　kidnap

II 次の語句を辞書で調べましょう。

　plot　　creature

⚰ *Enjoy the story!*

予習のための質問です。答えの参照となる英文部分を特定し、答えを日本語で準備しておきましょう。

1 What did Jonathan realize after he had seen the wolves leave licking their lips?
　狼たちが舌なめずりしながら去るのを見たあと、ジョナサンは何に気づいたか。

2 What gave Jonathan a dreadful sensation in the vault?
　ジョナサンが地下納骨堂でおぞましく感じたのはなぜか。

3 How had the Count changed when Jonathan saw him in the vault for the second time?
　ジョナサンが二度目に地下納骨堂で伯爵を見たとき伯爵はどう変化していたか。

4 What happened when Jonathan flung the shovel onto the Count?
　ジョナサンが伯爵にシャベルを振り下ろそうとしたとき何がおこったか。

5 What happened when Jonathan tried to escape through the open door?
　開いた扉からジョナサンが逃げようとしたとき何がおこったか。

In the vault

Jonathan Harker's diary

May 17th

   The Count told me to write three letters; one saying, "I have already finished my work in Transylvania and am leaving for London in a few days"; another saying, "I am leaving tomorrow"; and the last one saying, "I have arrived at Bistritz."

   I asked him what dates I should put. He said "June 12th, June 19th, and June 29th respectively." Now I know how long I am to live.

June 17th

   I heard some wagons arriving at the courtyard this morning. Looking out of the window, I saw two big wagons, each pulled by eight horses. Some Slovaks took a number of large boxes down from the wagons.

June 24th

   I now know the plot of the Count. I saw him crawling down again in my clothes, carrying the bag this time. He will snatch a child for the three women and post my letters. Local people will think the deed of kidnapping is my doing.

June 25th, morning

   Last night I heard a woman shouting, "Monster! Give my child back!" Then the Count uttered something at the window. I soon heard the familiar howling of wolves; hundreds of them were below. The woman stopped shouting and gave a sharp scream. A little later, I looked out of the window and saw wolves leave licking their lips. Then I heard the woman no more.

   Though I was horrified to death, I realized one thing: "Dreadful things happen only at night." The Count may sleep during the day. If so, I must get into his room before dark. But how?

   If the Count can crawl down the wall, I too should be able to crawl to his room

below mine. It is worth trying. Action!

Later, the same day

I have done it! I must write this down. At least, I won't just sit and wait for my death.

Since this castle is made of large stones, I could hold onto them and climb down to the window outside the Count's room. Just as I had hoped, the window was not locked. Inside the room, there was a spiral stairway. At its bottom was a long tunnel leading to a chapel, which, I could tell, was once a graveyard. The boxes I saw earlier were there — dozens of them. They were all full of earth which had been recently dug up from the graveyard ground in the chapel.

I went into the vault and made a discovery. In one of the boxes was lying the Count! I could not tell if he was awake or asleep, alive or dead. His eyes were open but not looking at anything. I touched his cheek, which was warm. His lips were red. But there was no breath, no beating of his heart. I began to look for the keys in his pockets. Then I felt a dreadful sensation. Though his eyes still looked lifeless, they showed such a hate that I could not remain there. I ran back to the stairway and climbed back to my room. I must think!

The Count leaves

Jonathan Harker's diary
29 June

Today is the date of the last letter. I saw the Count went out of the window in my clothes. I could not think about anything, so I went to the library and fell asleep.

Later the Count woke me up and said, "Tomorrow, my friend, you leave for England." I said, "Why not tonight?" He said, "It is because my coach and horses are away." I replied, "I am happy to leave on foot." Then, the Count said, "Come."

I followed him down to the front door and he opened it. I heard the howling of wolves nearby. It came closer and closer. I cried,

"Shut the door!"

Silently we returned to the library.

June 30th, morning

I woke up just before dawn. I felt safer when I saw the light coming into the room. I ran down to the entrance door. It was locked. I must get the keys!

I went to the vault. I felt myself shaking but I could not wait for another night. The box was in the same place, but there was the lid on it. I lifted the lid and was filled with horror. There lay the Count, but he looked younger. His hair and moustache, which had been white, were now dark grey. The cheeks were reddish, and the lips were unnaturally red.

"I am helping this horrible creature to come to London! There would be enough blood for this monster to live —among the millions of people forever!" I cried in my mind. I picked up a shovel near the box and tried to hit him. Then he turned his head towards me and stopped my motion with some mesmerising power. His eyes were surely staring at me and his sneer gave me a shudder! I flung the shovel down, but it only cut his forehead. I dropped the shovel.

Then I heard some men singing in Slovak. They were the men who came to pick up the boxes. I ran up to the Count's room and waited for them. I was going to run down and escape through the open door before they finished their job.

I dashed towards the door. But just then a gust of wind blew and shut the door with an echoing sound.

I'm a prisoner again. I would rather die than stay with those female monsters! I will try to climb down the wall and the precipice. But I'm sure I will fall before reaching the ground and die. Good bye, Mina! Good bye, all!

Ⅰ　1〜3と a)〜c) を組み合わせて3つの文を完成しなさい。

   1 When Jonathan found the Count in the box for the first time,

   2 Jonathan was horrified to see the Count

   3 Just as Jonathan was about to escape from the castle,

     a) he could not tell if the Count was alive or dead.

     b) a gust of wind shut the door.

     c) look younger with redder lips and darker hair.

Ⅱ　話の筋に沿って a)〜e) を並べ替えなさい。

    a) Jonathan heard a woman shout and then saw wolves leave licking their mouth.

    b) Jonathan wrote three letters as the Count requested him.

    c) Jonathan failed to destroy the Count with the shovel.

    d) Jonathan saw many big boxes arriving at the castle.

    e) Jonathan found the very box in which the Count was lying.

be 動詞 + to 不定詞　は予定、意図、義務、可能、運命などを表す。これらが複合する場合も多い。例えば次の文は、運命と可能を表し、またドラキュラから見た意図や予定を示唆する。

Now I know how long I *am to* live.　今や自分がどれだけ生きられるのか分かった。

■以下の2文を日本語に訳してみましょう。

   1) I am not to sit and wait for my death.

   2) I was not to tell if the Count in the coffin was alive or dead.

比較表現の例　would rather… than 〜　〜するより…するほうがましだ。／〜するよりむしろ…したい。

I *would rather* die *than* stay with those female monsters!

（あの女怪物たちといっしょにいるより死んだほうがましだ。）

■次の英文を完成しましょう。

   I [　　　　　　　　　] fall from the castle window [　　　　　] being a [　　　]!

   （幽閉の身でいるより城の窓から落ちたほうがましだ！）

enough A for B to 〜（B が〜するのに充分な A）

In London, there would be *enough blood for the Count to live on*.

（ロンドンには伯爵が存在するのに充分な血があるだろう。）

■空白に 6 語入れて英文を完成しましょう。

The Slovaks have brought [   ] place in several houses in London. （スロヴァキア人たちは伯爵がロンドンのいくつかの家に置くのに充分な（数の）箱を持ってきた。）

Listening in and acting out!

英語を聞いて会話を完成し、パートナーと口頭練習をしましょう。

A: Tomorrow, my friend, you leave for England.

B: [1   ] I think I'm overstaying your welcome.

A: It is because my coach and horses are away.

B: I would be [2   ].

A: Come, then. I'll show you the way out. You are [3   ].

原作にチャレンジ (3)

There, in one of the great boxes, of which there were fifty in all, on a pile of newly dug earth, lay the Count! He was either dead or asleep, I could not say which—for the eyes were open and stony, but without the glassiness of death—and the cheeks had the warmth of life through all their pallor, and the lips were as red as ever. But there was no sign of movement, no pulse, no breath, no beating of the heart. I bent over him, and tried to find any sign of life, but in vain. He could not have lain there long, for the earthy smell would have passed away in a few hours. By the side of the box was its cover, pierced with holes here and there. I thought he might have the keys on him, but when I went to search I saw the dead eyes, and in them, dead though they were, such a look of hate, though unconscious of me or my presence, that I fled from the place, and leaving the Count's room by the window, crawled again up the castle wall. Regaining my own chamber, I threw myself panting upon the bed and tried to think....

Chapter 4

死者たちの船

👤 *Get ready!*

授業に臨む準備をしましょう。

I 日本語と英語を一致させてください。

1 通信、手紙のやりとり　　2 発表する　　3 (結婚の) 申し込み

4 ネズミ算　　5 吐く　　6 廃墟の僧院　　7 重苦しい

8 巨大な　　9 航海日誌　　10 舵の柄

oppressive　　　proposal　　　log　　　correspondence

geometric progression　　　vomit　　　announce　　　gigantic

helm　　　ruined abbey

II 次の語句を辞書で調べましょう。

lunatic asylum（p.12 に既出）　　flirt（人を表す名詞として）　　suitor

case（人を表す名詞として）　　voyage

⚰️ *Enjoy the story!*

予習のための質問です。答えの参照となる英文部分を特定し、答えを日本語で準備しておきましょう。

1 What do you think Renfield did with the flies, spiders, and sparrows he had collected?
レンフィールドは、集めた蝿や蜘蛛や雀をどうしたと思うか。

2 Describe the port town of Whitby.
港町ホイットビーを描写しなさい。

3 Describe the beginning of the storm that arrived at Whitby.
ホイットビーに来た嵐の始まりを描写しなさい。

4 What did the log of the ship reveal?
船の航海日誌によって何が明らかになったか。

5 What did the captain look like when he was found on the ship?
船で発見されたとき船長はどんなようすだったか。

Lucy and her suitors

From the correspondence between Miss Mina Murray and Miss Lucy Westenra

May 9th

My dearest friend,

Forgive me, Lucy. I haven't written to you for a long time.

Jonathan has written so little to me from Transylvania. But he is well and returns in a week.

Tell me all what has happened to you since we saw each other last time. I have heard rumours about a tall handsome man.

Mina

Wednesday

My dearest Mina,

Don't tell me I haven't written to you about Arthur Holmwood. He is the handsome man you heard about. We have not announced yet, but we are engaged. The other day, he introduced a young doctor, John Seward to me. He is only 29 years old and directs a great lunatic asylum in London. He is a calm, intelligent person who would be perfect for you if you were not engaged with Jonathan.

Write to me soon.

Lucy

May 24th

Dear Mina.

It is so nice to be able to tell someone about Arthur, since we have kept our engagement secret.

Mina, you will not believe it, but I had a series of proposals today. The first one was from Dr Seward. I have already told you about him. He is very cool on the outside but has a very warm heart. Unfortunately, I had to say no to him. And Arthur came to make a formal proposal to me in my mother's presence. Of course, I accepted it, with Mother's permission this time. And then, later, an American fellow named Quincy Morris visited us and asked for my hand. He is nice and friendly, and very rich. But of course, I turned him down right away. Oh, do not think I am a terrible flirt but I wish I could marry all of them.

Lucy

Renfield and his geometric progression of life

Dr Seward's diary

June 5th

  To forget Lucy, I am concentrating on the study of a strange case. The more I understand this man named Renfield, the more interesting he grows to me. He has a great love for animals, but his pets are strange. Now he has collected a large quantity of flies. He says he is going to get rid of them soon.

July 1st

  Renfield now keeps spiders and feeds them with flies.

July 19th

  Renfield has collected lots of sparrows and feeds them with spiders. Today he asked me for "a big favour". I asked what he wanted and then he said, "A kitten. A nice playful kitten that I can feed and feed and feed." I was not surprised at his request, but I told him, "No".

July 20th

  I visited Renfield in his room this morning. His sparrows were gone and there were a few feathers around the room. He said the sparrows had escaped, but I saw bloodstains on his pillow.

  11 p.m.

  One of my staff came to notify me that Renfield had been very sick. He had vomited feathers.

Mina Murray's diary

July 24th, Whitby

  Whitby is a beautiful port town. On the precipice, between the ruined abbey and the town, there is a church with a big graveyard looking over the harbour. In fact, I am writing this diary on the bench among the old tombstones, enjoying the wonderful view. I am glad to stay with Lucy, but I wish Jonathan were with me, too. I wish he wrote to me, at least.

The Count arrives in England

Cutting from The Daily Telegraph, 8 August (pasted in Mina's Diary)

From a Correspondent, Whitby

Here in Whitby, there was one of the greatest storms on record. But this storm was peculiar.

It had been very hot and there had been no wind before the storm. In the afternoon, a report arrived from the coastguard that a storm was approaching. A little before 10 p.m. the air grew very oppressive, and the storm came with an incredible rapidity. The sea, which had been calm a moment before, was now full of gigantic waves. And a thickest fog ever experienced in this region came.

The coastguard used a searchlight to help the boats near the seashore. The light found a ship coming to the port. Everybody on the shore was afraid that it would hit the rocks. But soon a dense fog covered everything. Then suddenly, the wind changed the direction and blew away the fog. The next moment, we saw the ship quickly moving into the port.

What was more, the searchlight following the ship showed us a dead man. He was tied to the helm of the ship. His head went back and forth with the movement of the ship. The sight was horrible. Later the coastguard staff found that he was holding a crucifix.

The coastguard staff also reported that an extremely big dog landed when they started searching the deck. Soon they found the log of the ship. It revealed the presence of a strange man on the ship during its voyage. One by one the crew had died, till the captain tied himself to the helm. Only, he too was found dead as above reported.

I 1～3 と a)～c) を一致させて3つの文を完成しなさい。

1 Lucy was not unhappy to be courted by the three men
2 Renfield tried to take in as many lives as possible
3 The unusual storm and the dense fog probably

a) guided the ship into the port of Whitby.
b) though she was already engaged with Arthur Holmwood.
c) by starting with feeding spiders with flies.

II 話の筋に沿って a)～e) を並べ替えなさい。

a) A peculiar storm brought the ship with the dead captain and crew into the port of Whitby.
b) Lucy wrote about her fiancé Arthur and her other suitors in a letter to Mina.
c) The log of the ship revealed the presence of a strange man on the ship.
d) Renfield, having collected sparrows, asked for a kitten.
e) Renfield fell ill and vomited feathers.

Tips for reading

仮定法過去　過去形で、現代の事実に反する仮定や、ありそうにない事柄を表す。(be- 動詞の場合、3 人称単数も基本的には were となる)

Mina, *if you were not engaged* with Jonathan, Dr Seward *would* be perfect for you. （ミナ、あなたがジョナサンと婚約していなければ、セワード医師はあなたにまさにぴったりなのだけれど。）

I *wish* Jonathan *wrote* to me more. （ジョナサンがもっと手紙を書いてくれればいいのに。）

■次の英文を完成しましょう。

1) Mina says to herself, "I [　　　　　　　　　　　　] if Jonathan
[　　　　　　　　　　　　] with me now."
（「ジョナサンが今いっしょなら私はもっと幸せでしょうに」とミナは独りごちた。）

2) Lucy writes in her letter, "I wish I [　　　　　　　　　　] all the three men!"
（「3 人の男性みなと結婚できればいいのに」とルーシーは手紙に書いている。）

比較表現の例
The more I understand Renfield, *the more* interesting he grows to me.
（知れば知るほどレンフィールドは私にとって興味深くなる。）
What was more (=Furthermore / On top of that / To say more), the light

showed a dead man. (そのうえさらに、明かりで死者が見えた。)

■次の英文を完成しましょう。

1) The [   ] the monster takes in, the [   ] he
   becomes.
   (その怪物は、血を摂取すればするほど強くなる。)

2) Renfield collected sparrows, and [   ], he probably ate them.
   (レンフィールドは雀を集め、さらに言えば、おそらく雀たちを食べた。)

3) *Dracula* by Stoker has been read for more than a century.
   [   ], a number of films based on its story have been shot.
   (ストーカーの『ドラキュラ』は一世紀を超えて読み継がれている。さらに言えば、
   そのストーリーに基づいて多くの映画が撮られてきた。)

IT *Listening in and acting out!*

英語を聞いて会話を完成し、パートナーと口頭練習をしましょう。

A: I'm a reporter for The Daily Telegraph. Tell me. [1   ]
   at the port?

B: I saw a strange ship coming into the port [2   ]
   in the storm.

A: What happened, then?

B: Well, I think I saw [3   ] out of the ship as soon
   as it arrived.

A: Is it true that no one has survived on the ship?

B: Yes. We searched for survivors [4   ].

原作にチャレンジ (4)

It was no wonder that the coastguard was surprised, or even awed, for not often can such a sight have been seen. The man was simply fastened by his hands, tied one over the other, to a spoke of the wheel. Between the inner hand and the wood was a crucifix, the set of beads on which it was fastened being around both wrists and wheel, and all kept fast by the binding cords. The poor fellow may have been seated at one time, but the flapping and buffeting of the sails had worked through the rudder of the wheel and dragged him to and fro, so that the cords with which he was tied had cut the flesh to the bone.

Chapter 5

ルーシー、「侵入口」となる

👤 *Get ready!*

授業に臨む準備をしましょう。

Ⅰ　日本語と英語を一致させてください。

1 ほっとしている　　2（他者に）丁重である　　3 絶対的に
4 控える　　5 特定の　　6 専門知識　　7 食欲　　8 声をあげる
9 輸血　　10 麻酔薬

absolutely　　transfusion　　exclaim　　relieved　　respectful

expertise　　narcotic　　refrain　　specific　　appetite

Ⅱ　Google map でイングランドの港町 Whitby の位置を確認し、
　　ストリートビューの機能を使って廃墟の僧院や湾岸を見ましょう。

⚰ *Enjoy the story!*

予習のための質問です。答えの参照となる英文部分を特定し、答えを日本語で準備しておきましょう。

1 What did Mina see when she ran up the stairs of the East Cliff?
　ミナは東の崖の階段を駆け上がって何を見たか。

2 What was the news Mina received from Jonathan?
　ミナはジョナサンからどんな知らせを受けたか。

3 How did Dr Seward describe Van Helsing in the letter to Arthur Holmwood?
　アーサー・ホルムウッドへの手紙でセワード医師はヴァン・ヘルシングのことをどんな
　人物だと知らせたか。

4 Describe Lucy as Van Helsing and Dr Seward found her on September 7th.
　ヴァン・ヘルシングとセワード医師は9月7日にどのようなルーシーを目にしたか。

5 How did Van Helsing treat Lucy to save her?
　ヴァン・ヘルシングはルーシーを救おうとどのような治療を施したか。

On the East Cliff

(1-11)

Mina Murray's diary

August 11th, 3 a.m.

I'm at Lucy's at her request. I'm glad to be with her but I'm afraid for her, too. Lucy sleepwalked in her childhood for some time. Then she stopped. But she has started to sleepwalk again.

Earlier this evening, I suddenly woke up and looked around in our bedroom. Her bed was empty. I could not find her anywhere in the house. And I noticed the front door was open. I ran to the West Cliff and looked across the harbour to the East Cliff where Lucy and I often go to spend time. I saw someone dressed in white lying on the bench we often sat on together. The person looked like Lucy. And then I saw a man bending over her. Or, was it some beast?

I went down the stairs of the West Cliff and ran through the town street, and then ran up the stairs of the East Cliff. I could see something long and black was over her. I called out, "Lucy! Lucy! Lucy!" The long thing raised its head. I saw its white teeth and red eyes.

19世紀のホイットビー

When I reached her, she was alone breathing with difficulty. On the way home, I found two tiny points on her throat. They were bleeding a little. I must have pricked her throat by accident with the big safety pin when I put my shawl on her.

August 15th

Today Lucy's mother told me that Lucy was very ill. Her doctor said that her heart was so weak that it would not bear any excitement. I should not tell the old lady about Lucy's sleepwalking. Otherwise, her mother, who is also very weak, would fall in a serious condition from worrying.

Letter about the delivery of 50 boxes of earth to Carfax mansion written to Cater Paterson & Company

August 17th
Dear sirs,

Please deliver these 50 boxes to Carfax and place them in the underground old chapel of the mansion. We have enclosed the keys.

Faithfully yours,
Samuel Billington & Son, Solicitors

The first transfusion

Mina Murray's diary
August 19th

Oh, I'm so glad and relieved. At last I received a letter from Jonathan. He is in a hospital in Budapest. I will go there as soon as the train tickets are arranged. We should marry there. Mr. Hawkins, his employer, advised me to do so.

Dr Seward's diary
August 19th

A sudden change has been reported about Renfield. He had been respectful to my staff till yesterday, but this morning he told an attendant, "Go away! You are not important anymore. Master is near now."

Letter from Mina Harker to Lucy Westenra
August 24th, Budapest
Dearest Lucy,
I hope you are better now.

I am staying with Jonathan at a hospital in Budapest. He has greatly changed. A while ago, he asked me to find a notebook in his coat pocket. He said it contained all what had happened in the past few months. He has decided not to open the notebook unless the information in it is absolutely needed. He says he wants to restart his life with our marriage and forget his experiences in Transylvania. So, I will refrain myself from looking at it. We are going to marry this afternoon here in his hospital room.

Mina

Letter from Arthur Holmwood to Dr Seward

August 31st

My dear friend,

I need your help. Lucy is very ill with no specific disease. I know it is very difficult for you, but I must ask you to go to Whitby right away to save her. I will join you there as soon as possible.

Arthur

Letter from Dr Seward to Arthur Holmwood

September 2nd

Dear Arthur,

I examined Lucy, but I don't understand what exactly is wrong with her. I have already sent a telegram to Dr Van Helsing in Amsterdam asking him to come here quickly. He is an honoured professor and my master, well known for his expertise on strange diseases in the world. He is a warm-hearted person with a lot of courage.

Jack Seward

September 3rd

Dear Arthur,

Dr Van Helsing came and examined Lucy very carefully. When we were alone later, he told me that her situation was very serious. I asked what exactly he meant, but he just said he had to go back to the University of Amsterdam to collect some information to understand her disease better. Please be patient, Arthur. He will speak clearly as soon as he is ready.

Jack Seward

Telegrams from Dr Seward to Professor Van Helsing

4 September – Lucy is better.

5 September – Lucy has a good appetite. Her colour is coming back.

6 September – Terrible change. Come at once.

Dr Seward's diary
September 7th

As soon as Dr Van Helsing arrived, he asked me if I had said something to Arthur. I said no, and then he said, "He might not need to know. Or, he should know all. It all depends on what will happen from now."

We were shocked to see Lucy. The bones of her pale face were prominent. On leaving her room with me, the Professor exclaimed in a whispering voice. "This is horrible! We have no time to lose. We have to give her a transfusion immediately."

As soon as Arthur arrived, Dr Van Helsing gave Lucy a dose of a narcotic. Arthur kissed her on the forehead and Lucy fell into a deep sleep. Arthur, shocked to see Lucy, was willing to do anything to help her. The Professor performed a quick and accurate transfusion. As the blood left Arthur and entered Lucy's veins, Arthur looked happy but paler.

I 1〜3とa)〜c)を一致させて3つの文を完成しなさい。

1 Mina refrained from reading the notebook

2 A law firm arranged a delivery of 50 boxes

3 On the 6th of September, a terrible change for the worse occurred to Lucy,

  a) to the chapel of a mansion in London called Carfax.

  b) which contained the information on Jonathan's experiences in Transylvania.

  c) and Dr Van Helsing decided to give her a transfusion.

II 話の筋に沿ってa)〜e)を並べ替えなさい。

a) Mina married Jonathan at a hospital in Budapest.

b) Van Helsing examined Lucy and went back to Amsterdam to do more research on her illness.

c) Van Helsing gave a transfusion to Lucy using Arthur's blood.

d) Mina noticed that Lucy's bed was empty and found her on the East Cliff with a man or some beast.

e) Dr Seward did not understand Lucy's condition and sent a telegram to Van Helsing.

🦷 *Tips for reading*

完了助動詞　助動詞は話者の「現時点」での主観を表し、「have + 過去分詞」が続くと、それより前に起こったこと、もしくはそれまでに完了していることについての主観を表します。

I *must have pricked* her throat by accident.

（たまたま彼女の喉をついてしまったにちがいない。）

I *should have paid* more attention. (私はもっと注意を払うべきだった。)

■次の英文を完成しましょう。

1) The bed is empty. Lucy [　　　　　　　　　　] gone out.

（ルーシーは出て行ったにちがいない。）

2) Renfield acts strangely.　Something [　　　　　　　] happened to him.

（レンフィールドに何かが起こったのかもしれない。）

副詞節のなかの未来のことは現在形で、名詞節のなかの未来のことは未来形で表す。

As soon as the train tickets *are arranged*, I will go to Budapest.

（汽車の切符が用意でき次第、ブタペストに行きます。）

It all depends on what *will happen* from now. （すべてはこれから起こることにかかっている。）

■次の英文を完成しましょう。

1) Let me know when you [   ] at Budapest, Mina.
   （いつブタペストに着くのか知らせておくれ、ミナ。）
2) Let me know when you [   ] at Budapest, Mina.
   （ブタペストに着いたら知らせておくれ、ミナ。）
3) He will speak clearly as soon as he [   ] ready.
   （準備ができしだい明確に話してくれるでしょう。）

▐▊ *Listening in and acting out!*

英語を聞いて会話を完成し、パートナーと口頭練習をしましょう。

A: Have you said anything to your friend Arthur Holmwood?

B: No, I haven't let him know any of our opinions yet. Besides, I don't understand [1   ].

A: Very well. He might not need to know [2   ].
   Or, he should know all. It all depends on what will happen from now. (Both entering Lucy's room)

B: Oh! But⋯ this is horrible!

A: [3   ]! A transfusion, immediately!

(A maid opens the door and announces, "Sir Holmwood.")

B: Oh, Arthur has arrived.

A: [4   ] she needs his blood.

原作にチャレンジ (5)

　"He is so young and strong and of blood so pure that we need not defibrinate it." Then with swiftness, but with absolute method, Van Helsing performed the operation. As the transfusion went on something like life seemed to come back to poor Lucy's cheeks, and through Arthur's growing pallor the joy of his face seemed absolutely to shine. After a bit, I began to grow anxious, for the loss of blood was telling on Arthur, strong man as he was.

コラム2　『ドラキュラ』――執筆のきっかけとモデル

バーンベリ

『ドラキュラ』(1897) は東欧への旅で始まり東欧への旅で終わるが、この小説の執筆はそもそも、ハンガリー人の旅行家で著述家であるアールミン・バーンベリ (1832-1913) との出会いがきっかけだった。現スロヴァキアの地に生まれ、トルコに渡り、ペルシャを旅し、ブタペシュトで逝去した人物である。彼の話を聞いて外交官ウィルキンソンが書いた『ワラキアとモルダヴィアの領国（仮邦題）』

ヴラド3世

(*An Account of the Principalities of Wallachia and Moladavia*, 1820) を読んだことが、作者ストーカーの心を物語の舞台となる東欧の地に誘った。以来数年、仕事の合間をぬって大英博物館付属図書館（今の大英図書館）に通い、東欧の歴史と伝説を読み漁ることになる。

　『ドラキュラ伝説―吸血鬼のふるさとをたずねて』(*In Search

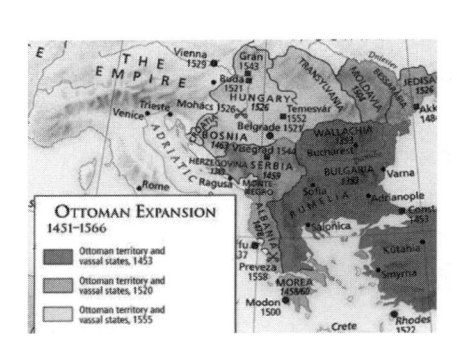

of Dracula, 1972, by Florescu and McNally）によればストーカーは、このリサーチで見出した15世紀のワラキア領主ワラキア公ヴラド3世（Vlad III Dracula, 1430/31- 1476）をドラキュラ伯爵の造形の基礎にしている。

　ワラキアは今のルーマニアの南部にあたる。当時ルーマニアはトランシルヴァニア(おおよそ今のハンガリー)、ワラキア、モルダヴィアに分かれていた。イスラムの覇者オスマン帝国との戦いの前線に位置し、その支配下に置かれたときもあった。父ヴラド2世がオスマンに勝利したことで神聖ローマ帝国皇帝からドラゴンの騎士団に叙され、ドラクルと名乗るようになる。ヨーロッパではイングランドを始め、多くの国や地域が、ドラゴンを退治する聖ジョージを守護聖人としているが、ドラゴン騎士団に

リュブリャナのドラゴン

属する領主が統治した中東欧の地域では今もドラゴンを守りの象徴とするところが少なくない。たとえばスロベニアの首都リュブリャナの城壁を守るのはドラゴンである。

　ヴラド3世は「ヴラド・ツェペシェ（串刺し王）」と渾名されるが、それはオスマンの兵士ばかりか、味方側の兵士や側近までを生きながら串刺しにして野外に晒したからだそうだ。今に残る「串刺し」の逸話は、勇猛果敢なイス

16世紀の木版画

ラムの軍勢は言うにおよばず、連合勢力内の裏切りも視野に入れ、残虐な評判を広める
ことで内外の敵を威嚇しておく心理情報作戦の名残りだと考えられる。じっさい父ヴラ
ド 2 世はハンガリー王に裏切られて亡命したことがあった。物語『ドラキュラ』も後半
は情報作戦となり、さらにこの串刺しが逆にドラキュラ伯爵を退治するイメージに使わ
れている。またヴラド 3 世は、戦死が伝えられても地中から蘇るドラゴンのように神出
鬼没に戦ったと報告されており、その姿は生き血で幾度も蘇る
ドラキュラ伯爵に通じる。

　ところで、ドラキュラ伯爵の素材はヴラド 3 世だけではない
ようだ。その造形には、自らの野心を精力的に実現するなか、
個人秘書かつ劇団マネージャーであるストーカーに、広報、会
計、脚本の選定と執筆、ときには端役まで、次々と業務の遂行
を求めたヘンリー・アーヴィングの面影も反映されているので
はないだろうか。当然、舞台でドラキュラ役を演じてヒットさ
せ、ストーカーを「海外遠征」に連れ出したのもこの男であった。

アーヴィング

参考文献 *From the Shadow of Dracula: A Life of Bram Stoker*
(Paul Murray, Jonathan Cape, Publisher, 2004)

Chapter 6

ルーシー、「戦場」となる

👤 *Get ready!*

授業に臨む準備をしましょう。

I 日本語と英語を一致させてください。

1 ～に値する　　2（針などで）あいた穴　　3 取ってくる
4 生き返らせる　5 無意識の　　6 懐疑主義者
7 功績、功績に基く信用　　8 充血した　9 パタパタという音　10 巨大な

enormous　　fetch　　sceptic　　blood-shot　　revive
unconscious　　flapping　　deserve　　puncture　　credit

II 次の語句を辞書で調べましょう。

instrument　　superstition　　get rid of　　speck

⚰ *Enjoy the story!*

予習のための質問です。答えの参照となる英文部分を特定し、答えを日本語で準備しておきましょう。

1 When the black band around Lucy's neck moved, what did Van Helsing and Dr Seward notice?
ルーシーの首の黒いバンドがずれたとき、ヴァン・ヘルシングとセワード医師は何に気づいたか。

2 What did Van Helsing give to Lucy on the 11th of September?
ヴァン・ヘルシングは9月11日、ルーシーに何を与えたか。

3 What did Lucy's mother do with the flowers?
ルーシーの母は花をどうしたか。

4 What happened in front of the wolf cage of the Zoological Garden on the 17th of September?
動物園の狼の檻の前で9月17日、何がおこったか。

5 What happened after the head of a giant wolf had broken through the window pane of Lucy's bedroom?
大きな狼の頭部がルーシーの寝室の窓ガラスを破ったあと、何がおこったか。

The Professor researches

Dr Seward's diary

September 7th

When the transfusion was finished, Van Helsing said, "Now the brave lover deserves a kiss." When Arthur kissed Lucy on her cheek, a narrow black band around her neck moved. Her fiancé did not see, but Van Helsing and I noticed the two red marks on her throat.

As soon as Arthur went down to take some port wine to warm his body, we examined the marks. There was a tiny puncture in each of them. Do these punctures have anything to do with her loss of blood? But if so, there must be bloodstains on her pillow.

The Professor said that he must go back to Amsterdam to fetch some books and instruments he needed. "You stay here and watch her every second tonight," he added.

September 8th

Last night I was awake all night by her bed. This morning, she woke up in a better condition.

I noticed this evening that every time she was about to fall asleep she forced herself to stay awake. I asked her, "Don't you like to go to sleep?" She replied, "I am afraid of sleeping." "Why? I like sleeping. It revives me." "You wouldn't if you were like me. It is the beginning of horror," she answered. I asked what she meant but she only shook her head. So, I assured her, "I promise you. If I see you having a bad dream, I will wake you up." Then her face lit up. "Oh, will you? Will you, please? Then I will sleep." Saying this, she fell asleep.

September 9th

"Mr. Seward, you don't have to stay awake for me tonight. Next to this room, there is a nice cosy room you can sleep in. I will call you if I have any problem," Lucy said to me. I accepted this offer since I was so tired. I wasn't sure if I could stay awake in her room, anyway.

September 10th

The Professor put his hand on my shoulder and woke me up. "How is our patient?" he asked. "She was well last night," I answered and we both went

into her room. The room was dark with the blind down. I pulled it up and let the light in. "My God!" The Professor pointed to the bed. Lucy was lying there but looked awfully pale and unconscious. "Quick! She needs another transfusion. You have to give her your blood."

September 11th

When I went to Lucy's room this afternoon, I found her better and the Professor happier. A big white box had arrived for him. He opened it and I saw it was full of white flowers in the form of a loose wreath.

"For you, Lucy." The Professor handed them to Lucy.

She smelt them and winced. "Are you joking me, Professor? These are garlics." To my surprise, Van Helsing became angry and declared to Lucy. "I never joke, Miss Westenra. I'm doing my best to save you. Don't block my efforts!" Then he saw Lucy was frightened and said calmly, "Don't be afraid. Everything I do here is for your sake."

I said, "Well, Professor, I know that you always have a scientific reason for your words and actions. But a sceptic would think you are using magic or believe in superstitions."

"Maybe I am," said the Professor.

The Count's last visit

Dr Seward's diary (continued)

September 13th

Van Helsing and I went to see Lucy at eight o'clock in the morning. Lucy's mother met us in the hall and said, "Lucy is better now." The Professor said smiling, "Then our medicine worked well." The old lady said, "Don't take all the credit, Professor. I helped my daughter, too." "What do you mean?" I asked. "Well, last night, there was a terrible smell in her room, so I got rid of the flowers."

The moment he heard this, he dashed to Lucy's room. I followed him and saw him trying to control himself. "God! God! What have we done?" Then we

prepared another transfusion. The Professor himself gave her blood this time.

Article from The Pall Mall Gazette (later pasted in Mina's diary)
September 18.

From the interview with the keeper at the Zoological Garden about the escaped wolf.

Last evening, there was a strange man in front of the wolf cage. He was a thin, tall man with awfully blood-shot eyes. "The wolves are upset about something," said the man to the keeper. He answered, "Maybe it's you, sir." Then the man said, "They never hurt me," and smiled showing long white teeth. Later, around midnight, the keeper found the biggest wolf was gone.

Memorandum left by Lucy Westenra

I must write down what I remember about tonight while I can, because I don't want to cause trouble to anyone. I wish Dr Seward were with us now. Professor Van Helsing sent a telegram to him two days ago, but Dr Seward hasn't arrived yet.

I went to bed with the flower wreath and fell asleep before long. But I woke up because of some flapping at the window. I heard a weird howling, too. I looked out of the window and only saw a bat. Oh, but it was a bat of an enormous size! I went back to bed. The flapping and the howling were getting more frequent. Mother was sleeping in the same room. She was more afraid than I was. Poor Mother!

The flapping continued and there was a crash. The head of a gigantic wolf had broken through the window pane. Mother pointed at it for a few seconds and fell over dead on top of me. A lot of little specks came into the room. They were turning around in circle and began to make a silhouette of a man. I don't remember what happened then. I must have fainted.

Mother is gone. I'm alone with her and I don't know how long I will be alive, for I feel so weak.

May God protect you, Arthur!

Ⅰ 1〜3とa)〜c)を組み合わせて3つの文を完成しなさい。

1 Lucy tried to stay awake

2 Professor Van Helsing got angry

3 A thin tall man had been seen in front of the wolf cage of the Zoological Garden

   a) before a gigantic wolf broke through the window pane of Lucy's bedroom.

   b) when Lucy complained of the garlic flowers.

   c) because she was afraid of having a horrible dream.

Ⅱ 話の筋に沿ってa)〜e)を並べ替えなさい。

   a) Lucy's mother took the wreath of garlic flowers off her daughter, which led to another transfusion.

   b) Van Helsing noticed the punctures on Lucy's throat and went back to Amsterdam to fetch some books and instruments.

   c) Dr Seward slept in the room next to Lucy's and later found that she had lost blood during the night.

   d) A big bat came to the window of Lucy's bedroom and a gigantic wolf broke into it.

   e) Dr Van Helsing gave a wreath of garlic flowers to Lucy so that she could sleep safely.

🦷 *Tips for reading*

have 〜 to do with…「関係がある、ない」の表現
Do these punctures *have anything to do with* her loss of blood?
（これらの穴は彼女の失血と何か関係があるのか。）

■英文を、選択肢の語を使って完成しましょう。

1) The fact that Lucy sleepwalked in her childhood had [   ] to do with her peculiar condition. （ほとんど関係ない）

2) Seward suspected that the strange gift of garlic flowers had [   ] to do with Lucy's peculiar condition. （何か関係がある）

3) Probably the Professor suspected that the punctures on the throat had [   ] to do with the loss of blood. （大いに関係がある）

選択肢 much / little / something

省略の例

I found Lucy better and (I found) the Professor happier.

（ルーシーは具合が良くなり、教授は嬉しそうだった。）

while「〜する間」、as if「まるで」、to 不定詞の to の後、関係副詞の先行詞などもしばしば省略

While (I was) riding in the Count's coach, I saw some blue flames.

The punctures were white as if (they were) suppurated.

（穴はまるで膿んでいるかのように白かった。）

The Count cannot enter a house unless someone inside permits him to (enter).

（伯爵は、誰か中の人が入るのを許可しないと入ることはできない。）

We found a child (at the spot) where something white had moved.

（先に何か白いものが動いた場所で子どもを見つけた。）

■日本語にしましょう。

　Arthur showed his love, Mina her courage, and the Professor his expertise.

祈願文　May 〜！「〜でありますように！」

May God protect Arthur!　（アーサーに神のご加護を！）

■次の英文を完成しましょう。

　May you [　　　　　　　　　　　]! （あなたが幸せでありますように！）

　[　　　　　] the soul of Lucy's mother rest in peace!

　（ルーシーの母の魂が安らかでありますように！）

IT **_Listening in and acting out!_**

英語を聞いて会話を完成し、パートナーと口頭練習をしましょう。

I　A: So Lucy is better now? Then [1　　　　　　　　　　　　　　　].

　B: Don't [2　　　　　　　　　], Professor. I helped my daughter, too.

　A: What do you mean?

　B: Well, last night, there was a terrible smell in her room, so [3　　　　　　　　　].

　A: God! Oh, no! What have we done?

II　A: Sir, the garden is closing now. Why are you [1　　　　　　　　　　　]?

　B: They are [2　　　　　　　　　].

　A: Maybe they are upset about you, sir.

　B: [3　　　　　　　　　]. They never hurt me.

Memorandum left by Lucy Westenra.

I write this and leave it to be seen, so that no one may by chance get into any trouble through me. This is an exact record of what took place tonight. I feel I am dying of weakness, and have barely strength to write, but it must be done if I die in the doing.

I went to bed as usual, taking care that the flowers were placed as Dr. Van Helsing directed, and soon fell asleep.

I was waked by the flapping at the window, which had begun after the sleep-walking on the cliff at Whitby when Mina saved me, and which now I know so well. I was not afraid, but I did wish that Dr. Seward was in the next room—as Dr. Van Helsing said he would be—so that I might have called him. I tried to go to sleep, but could not. Then there came to me the old fear of sleep, and I determined to keep awake. Perversely sleep would try to come when I did not want it; so, as I feared to be alone, I opened my door and called out: "Is there anybody there?" There was no answer. I was afraid to wake mother, and so closed my door again. Then outside in the shrubbery I heard a sort of howl like a dog's, but more fierce and deeper. I went to the window and looked out, but could see nothing, except a big bat, which had evidently been buffeting its wings against the window.

Chapter 7

不死者ルーシー

🪦 *Get ready!*

授業に臨む準備をしましょう。

I 日本語と英語を一致させてください。

1 気持ちの動揺　　2 化膿している　　3 つぶやく　　4 官能を求めるような
5 出くわす　　6 亡くなる　　7 墓場　　8 墓石　　9 唸る　　10 棺

pass away　　graveyard　　tomb　　emotions　　coffin
come across　　groan　　suppurated　　murmur　　voluptuous

II　次の語句を辞書で調べましょう。

check（動詞）　　the undead

⚰️ *Enjoy the story!*

予習のための質問です。答えの参照となる英文部分を特定し、答えを日本語で準備しておきましょう。

1 What did Lucy's face look like when Van Helsing and Dr Seward broke into her room?
　ヴァン・ヘルシングとセワード医師がルーシーの部屋に押し入ったとき、ルーシーはどんな面相だったか。

2 What was "Hampstead Mystery" reported in *The Westminster Gazette*?
　ウエストミンスター・ガゼット紙の報じる「ハムステッドの謎」とはどんな出来事か。

3 What stopped Jonathan from going out?
　なぜジョナサンは外出しなかったのか。

4 What did Dr Seward and Van Helsing see and find at the graveyard on the 26th of September?
　セワード医師とヴァン・ヘルシングは、９月２６日、墓場で何を見て、また何を見つけたのか。

5 What does Arthur have to do with Lucy's body in the coffin, according to Van Helsing?
　ヴァン・ヘルシングによれば、アーサーは棺の中のルーシーの遺体をどうすべきか。

Lucy Passes Away

Dr Seward's diary
September 19th

I received a telegram from Van Helsing only yesterday morning. He was worried because Lucy had to spend a night alone with her mother last night. We hurried to their house and knocked on the door. But no one answered. We broke the lock and ran up to Lucy's bedroom. I cannot describe the scene without emotions.

The two women were lying down on the bed. The old lady was covered with a white sheet. But Lucy was not. Her eyes were open and there was a look of horror in them. The garlic flowers were cast on the floor. The punctures on her throat were torn. They were so white as if suppurated. The Professor bent over Lucy and listened to her heart. Then he cried out, "Brandy! Transfusion! Quick!"

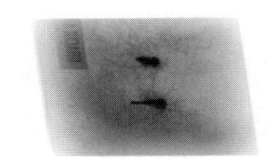

September 20th

We spent the night by Lucy. At six, the Professor started to examine her carefully in the morning light. The holes on her throat had disappeared. "She is dying. Call Mr. Arthur Holmwood here," he gravely murmured.

When Arthur arrived, Lucy suddenly opened her eyes and called to him, "Arthur, Arthur, please come to me and kiss me." The Professor checked him saying, "No. Not yet!"

"Arthur!" Now her voice was strangely voluptuous. Arthur was about to kiss her when the Professor pushed him away. I saw a rage in Lucy's face. But she closed her sharp teeth with force to conceal them. A moment later, she opened her eyes again and held the Professor's hand. She calmly said, "Thank you, sir." She breathed with difficulty for a while and then stopped breathing.

"We have to be brave to give her peace," said the Professor.

"What do you mean? She is dead and in peace now," said I.

"We'll have to wait and see," he replied.

Lucy, the undead

An article from The Westminster Gazette (kept by Van Helsing)
September 25th

In Hampstead, a suburb of London, more than ten children have returned home much later than usual or have not returned. Those who have returned say they came across a lady, who kissed them. They all have punctures on the throat. Some say that "the lady" the children met was perhaps a big rat or a dog. But others take this incident very seriously and named it Hampstead Mystery.

Letter from Van Helsing to Mina Harker
September 24th
Dear Madam,

I am Professor Van Helsing who was with Lucy when she passed away. Arthur Holmwood gave me permission to go through her correspondence and I found your letters. I will come to Exeter to see you tomorrow without waiting for your answer. And please do not tell your husband. I do not want to upset him.

Sincerely yours,
Van Helsing

Mina Harker's diary
September 25th

I had a meeting with Professor Van Helsing. What a meeting! I gave him my diary so that he could read what had happened to Lucy. Then it occurred to me that he might be able to help Jonathan. Jonathan is so afraid that he doesn't go out at all. He says he saw Count Dracula in London. I gave his diary to the Professor, too. He began to read it right away in front of me.

Dr Seward's diary
September 26th

A week ago, I thought everything was over. But now it has started again.

Renfield has collected flies. Today he started to collect spiders.

Arthur is doing okay considering his loss. His best friend Quincy Morris is with him.

As for me, I am trying to forget Lucy, but it is not finished yet. Today, the Professor came to my office and showed me an article about the children with punctures on their throat. "What do you think about this article?" he asked me.

"It reminds me of Lucy's case. Whatever left those punctures on the children also left the punctures on Lucy's neck," I answered. Then the Professor commented, "You are correct in a way, but not completely. And it is much worse." "What do you mean?" I shouted, because I was imagining something horrible.

The Professor looked at me calmly and said, "I hope you have the courage to come to the graveyard with me. We will check Lucy's tomb. Then, you will know."

We secretly went to Lucy's tomb. From 10 p.m., we waited and waited outside the tomb. Suddenly, something white moved under the yew trees. But it disappeared as soon as it noticed us. We found a child lying where the white thing had moved. "No. It's impossible," I groaned. But I knew it was true.

September 27th

We returned to Lucy's tomb. The Professor opened the coffin. Lucy was lying there more beautiful than ever. The Professor showed me her pointed teeth. He said, "Lucy is now 'the undead'. We have to cut off her head and fill her mouth with garlic. But we must have Arthur do this. Otherwise, he would think we killed her."

イチイの木 (yew tree): 枝が横に伸びて墓石を守る

I 1～3 と a)～c) を組み合わせて 3 つの文を完成しなさい。

1 Van Helsing stopped Arthur

2 Jonathan was afraid and could not go out

3 Dr Seward did not want to believe

a) what he imagined about Lucy after her "death".

b) from kissing Lucy on her deathbed.

c) because he believed to have seen Count Dracula in London.

II 話の筋に沿って a)～e) を並べ替えなさい。

a) Mina Harker met Van Helsing and handed to him Jonathan's diary as well as hers.

b) Van Helsing and Dr Seward found Lucy in her coffin lying more beautiful than ever.

c) The Westminster Gazette reported that more than ten children were missing or came back late with some punctures on the neck.

d) Van Helsing and Seward went to the graveyard and saw something white move.

e) Van Helsing and Seward found Lucy's mother dead and Lucy dying in her bedroom.

Tips for reading

目的を導く so that (that を省略することがある。稀に so を省略することもある。)

Mina gave the Professor her diary *so (that)* he could read what had happened to Lucy.

(前にルーシーに何が起こったか読めるように、ミナは自分の日記を教授に渡した。)

「程度・因果」で呼応する so …that ～

Jonathan was *so* afraid *that* he wouldn't go out at all.

(ジョナサンは怖がってまったく出かけない / まったく出かけないほど怖がっていた。)

■次の文を完成しましょう。

1) Dr Seward was [　　　　　　　　　] he could not describe Lucy without emotions. (セワード医師はショックを受けて動揺せずにルーシーを描写できなかった。)

2) Renfield collected flies [　　　　　　　　　] he could feed them to spiders.

(レンフィールドは、蜘蛛に与えることができるよう蠅を集めた。)

3) Arthur writes, "I need facts [　　　　　] my imagination [　　　　　　] get out of control."

(「想像が制御できなくならないように事実が要る」とアーサーは記している。)

使役・依頼の have＋ 目的語＋動詞の原形
We must *have Arthur do* this.
（これはアーサーにやらせねばならない。／やってもらわねばならない。）

■次の英文を完成しましょう。
The Professor [　　　] Dr Seward [　　　　　　] with him to the graveyard.
（教授はセワード医師をいっしょに墓場へ来させた。）

名詞節、副詞節を導く whatever の例
Whatever left those punctures on the children also left the punctures on Lucy's neck.
（子どもたちにあの穴を残したものがなんであろうと（それが）ルーシーの首にも穴を残した。 ―名詞節）
Whatever happens to Mina, she is ready to cope with it.
（自分に何が起ころうと、ミナには対応する覚悟がある。 ―副詞節）

■次の英文を日本語に訳しましょう。
1) Whatever he does is for Lucy's own sake.（whatever は名詞節中の目的語）
2) Whatever he does, he does it for Lucy's own sake.（whatever は副詞節中の目的語）
3) Whatever occurred to the ship was the Count's doing.（whatever は名詞節中の主語）

II **Listening in and acting out!**

英語を聞いて会話を完成し、パートナーと口頭練習をしましょう。
A: [1　　　　　　　　　　　　　　　　] this article?
B: It reminds me of Lucy's case. [2　　　　　　　　　　] on the children also left the punctures on Lucy's neck.
A: You are correct in a way, but not completely. [3　　　　　　　　].
B: What do you mean?
A: I believe [4　　　　　　　　　　] come to the graveyard with me tonight. We will check Lucy's tomb. Then, you will know.

原作にチャレンジ (7)

  And then insensibly there came the strange change which I had noticed in the night. Her breathing grew stertorous, the mouth opened, and the pale gums, drawn back, made the teeth look longer and sharper than ever. In a sort of sleep-waking, vague, unconscious way she opened her eyes, which were now dull and hard at once, and said in a soft voluptuous voice, such as I had never heard from her lips:

"Arthur! Oh, my love, I am so glad you have come! Kiss me!" Arthur bent eagerly over to kiss her; but at that instant Dr Van Helsing, who, like me, had been startled by her voice, swooped upon him, and catching him by the neck with both hands, dragged him back with a fury of strength. I never thought he could have possessed such a strength and he actually hurled Arthur almost across the room.

"Not for your life!" he said; "not for your living soul and hers!" And he stood between them like a lion at bay.

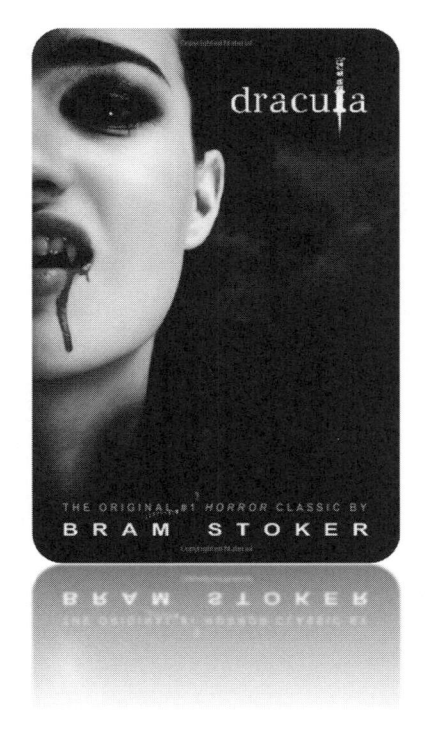

Chapter 8

ヴァン・ヘルシングの分析と戦略

🎩 *Get ready!*

授業に臨む準備をしましょう。

I 日本語と英語を一致させてください。

1 残酷な　　2 死装束　　3 悪魔的な　　4 変装する　　5 戦略

6 あり場所　　7 ひたすら（じいっと）　　8 殲滅する　　9 動員する　　10 消毒する

mobilize　　sterilize　　cruel　　shroud　　diabolical

whereabouts　　intently　　strategy　　annihilate　　disguise

II 次の語句を辞書で調べましょう。

sacred wafer　　　transform

⚰ *Enjoy the story!*

予習のための質問です。答えの参照となる英文部分を特定し、答えを日本語で準備しておきましょう。

1 What did Lucy look like when she appeared at the graveyard?
　墓場に姿を現したとき、ルーシーはどんなようすだったか。

2 What shocked Dr Seward?
　セワード医師は何に衝撃を受けたか。

3 What did Van Helsing regard as the strength of Count Dracula?
　And what did he regard as the advantages of his team in confronting Count Dracula?
　ヴァン・ヘルシングは、ドラキュラの強みは何だと見なしたか。
　また、ドラキュラに対峙するときの自分たちの強みは何だと見なしたか。

4 What did Van Helsing propose doing with the large boxes?
　ヴァン・ヘルシングは大きな箱をどうしようと提案したか。

5 Why did Van Helsing decide to leave Mina behind?
　ヴァン・ヘルシングがミナを同行させないと決めたのはなぜか。

Setting Lucy free

Dr Seward's diary
September 29th

Van Helsing explained to Arthur and Quincy about "the undead". He also gave Arthur the details of what he had to do to Lucy in order to save her soul. Arthur was upset and furious at the beginning. We laid out in front of him all the facts we had collected about Lucy, including her memorandum. In the end, he understood.

When the four of us reached her tomb, the Professor asked me if the body of Lucy had been in the coffin the previous night. I answered yes. Then we opened her coffin. It was empty.

Next, the Professor put pieces of sacred wafer around the entrance of the tomb. Quincy looked at him questioningly. The Professor said to him, "I am closing the tomb so that the undead should not enter it."

We waited for Lucy behind some yew trees. She appeared after a while. That sweet Lucy now looked cruel and voluptuous. On her chin and her white shroud were some bloodstains.

Seeing us, she stopped and made a sound like that of an angry cat. She saw Arthur and said, "Come. Come to me, Arthur, my husband." Her voice was diabolical but carried a streak of sweetness. The moment Arthur stepped forward to her she jumped to him. Before Lucy could kiss Arthur, however, the Professor, holding a crucifix, had placed himself between them. She quickly disappeared into the darkness. Arthur covered his face with his hands and whispered, "Let us do what we have to do." The Professor took off the sacred wafer from the entrance of the tomb.

The following day we went back to her tomb. Lucy was in her coffin, as beautiful as ever. I wondered if the thing we had seen the previous night was Lucy or some demon disguised as her. The Professor said, "We must set Lucy free." Arthur agreed to his words and put the point of the stake over her heart. He hit it with the hammer as hard as he could. We all said a prayer for her.

Arthur was shedding tears. The thing in the coffin moved about and gave out horrible screams. Finally, it stopped moving. Then, we saw the sweet Lucy we knew lying there.

Working out a strategy

Dr Seward's diary
September 30th

Jonathan Harker arrived at the asylum and joined us today. If what his diary tells us is true, he must be very brave. Then he and his wife Mina went into their room. I now hear the noise of the typewriter. Mina is knitting together all the pieces of the information and evidence we have. We came to know about the Count's boxes and their whereabouts. I was shocked to know that some of the boxes are now in Carfax right next to this asylum. But it explains the strange behaviour of Renfield.

The same day, in the afternoon

Mina Harker asked me to let her see Renfield. "What you have written down about him interests me," she said.

I told Renfield that there was a lady who wanted to see him. Then he asked me to give a few moments to tidying up his room. He collected all the spiders scattered on the floor and swallowed them.

Mina went into his room and said, "Good afternoon, Mr. Renfield. Dr Seward has told me of you." Renfield looked at Mina intently and, to my embarrassment, he said, "You are not the girl Dr Seward wanted to marry." Mina said smiling at him, "Oh, I have a husband. How are you?" Renfield said to Mina, "Then, don't stay."

Mina answered, "I hope I will see you in a happier condition. Take care!" "Good bye. May God protect you!" replied Renfield.

Mina Harker's diary
September 30th

Today, we all met in Dr Seward's study. We had to decide how we were going to fight the Count. Arthur, Mr. Quincy, Dr Seward, Jonathan and I were at the table and listened to Professor Van Helsing. The Professor had made a thorough research in Amsterdam about the Count.

"Vampires get more power as they suck blood. The vampire, Count Dracula, who we must annihilate is as strong as twenty men. He is very clever and can mobilize the dead. He can command animals like rats, bats, and wolves. He can transform himself into those animals as well as the form of speckles or fog. He can cause a gust of wind and a thunder. He is as powerful an enemy as we can imagine."

"But we also have advantages. We have love and friendship, and science. We can act night and day while the Count cannot act during the day. We are free while he is not; when he visits a house for the first time, he cannot enter it unless somebody inside permits him to. In addition, certain things hurt him, such as garlic and a crucifix. He cannot cross running waters unless someone carries him. And we can kill him by cutting his head off the body and driving a stake through his heart."

The Professor continued, "First, we must find all the boxes he sleeps in during the day. They contain the decayed earth from the old graves in the castle. We must sterilize all the boxes by putting a piece of sacred wafer in each of them so that he has no place to hide in. Then we must find him between sunrise and sunset."

I was ready to fight the Count together with the others. But the Professor told me, "From now on, Mrs. Harker, we will not let you know anything about this fight until the Count is dead. We can fight better when we know you are not in danger with us."

Now all the men have gone to Carfax to look for the boxes.

I 1〜3とa)〜c) を組み合わせて3つの文を完成しなさい。

　1 Arthur drove a stake into Lucy's body

　2 The Count cannot enter a house he visits for the first time

　3 Though Mina was ready to join the men in the fight,

　　a) she was left behind in the asylum.

　　b) so that her soul should be saved.

　　c) unless someone inside lets him in.

II　話の筋に沿ってa)〜e) を並べ替えなさい。

　a) Van Helsing explained to the men and Mina how they could fight the Count.

　b) The men waited for Lucy to appear outside the tomb.

　c) The men found Lucy in the coffin as beautiful as ever.

　d) When the Professor and the others opened Lucy's coffin, it was empty.

　e) Arthur drove a stake into Lucy's body.

対比を表す while

We can act night and day *while* the Count can act only during the night.

（伯爵は夜だけしか動けないが、われわれは昼夜動ける。）

■次の英文を完成しましょう。

　We are free [　　　] Dracula is [　　　].

　（ドラキュラが自由でない一方我々は自由だ / 我々は自由であるがドラキュラは自由ではない。）

as… as ever「相変わらず」　　more …than ever 「それまで（これまで）以上に」

Lucy was in the coffin, *as beautiful as ever*.

（ルーシーは棺の中にいた。相変わらず美しいままで。）

■次の英文を完成しましょう。

　1) The Count was [　　　　　　　　　].

　（伯爵には相変わらず力があった (powerful)。）

　2) Lucy was lying in the coffin [　　　　　　　　].

　（ルーシーはそれまで以上に美しく棺に横たわっていた。）

最上級を意味する as … as ～

He is *as powerful an enemy as* we can imagine.
(奴はわれわれが想像できる限り最強の敵である。)
＜参考＞　as…as any（どの～よりも）　He is as powerful as any other enemy.

■次の英文を完成しましょう。
　Lucy in the graveyard looked [　　　　　　　] she had ever looked.
　（墓場のルーシーは、それまでの彼女で最も官能を求めているように (voluptuous) に見えた。）

Listening in and acting out!

英語を聞いて会話を完成し、パートナーと口頭練習をしましょう。
　A: Good afternoon, Mr. Renfield. Dr Seward [1　　　　　　　　　].
　B: You are not the girl Dr Seward wanted to marry, are you?
　A: Oh, I'm married. How are you?
　B: Then, [2　　　　　　　　]. Leave this place now.
　A: I hope I will see you [3　　　　　　　]. Take care!
　A: Good bye. [4　　　　　　]!

原作にチャレンジ (8)

She walked over to him, smiling pleasantly, and held out her hand.

"Good evening, Mr. Renfield," said she. "You see, I know you, for Dr Seward has told me of you." He made no immediate reply, but eyed her all over intently with a set frown on his face. This look gave way to one of wonder, which merged in doubt; then, to my intense astonishment, he said:"You're not the girl the doctor wanted to marry, are you? You can't be, you know, for she's dead." Mrs. Harker smiled sweetly as she replied:"Oh no! I have a husband of my own, to whom I was married before I ever saw Dr Seward, or he me. I am Mrs. Harker."

"Then what are you doing here?"

"My husband and I are staying on a visit with Dr Seward."

"Then don't stay."

Chapter 9

ミナの危機

授業に臨む準備をしましょう。日本語と英語を一致させてください。

1 悪臭　　2 宥めるように　　3 崇める　　4 固体の　　5 ぎょっとして
6 大きく吐く　　7 危機　　8 ひざまずく　　9 嘆き悲しむ　　10 息をのむ

peril　　kneel　　odour　　solid　　alerted
heave　　soothingly　　worship　　gasp　　grieving

Enjoy the story!

予習のための質問です。答えの参照となる英文部分を特定し、答えを日本語で準備しておきましょう。

1 How many boxes were found at Carfax? What were the "hundreds of red points" that appeared there?
カーファクス邸で箱はいくつ見つかったか。そこに現れた「何百もの赤い点」は何か。

2 Why did the confession of Renfield alert the men?
なぜ男たちはレンフィールドの告白にぎょっとしたのか。

3 What was Count Dracula doing to Mina Harker when the men broke into the room?
男たちが部屋に押し入ると、ドラキュラ伯爵はミナに何をしていたか。

4 Why did the mist give Mina Harker a shudder?
なぜミナは霧に怖気を感じたのか。

5 What made Jonathan Harker groan?
なぜジョナサン・ハーカーは呻いたのか。

The confession of Renfield

🎧 2-6

Jonathan Harker's diary
October 1st, 5 a.m.

I felt relieved to leave Mina at the asylum. I didn't want her to take part in this horrible business.

Quincy showed a silver whistle to us. "Carfax will be full of rats. If they appear, I will blow my whistle and my dogs will come." Then the Professor gave each of us a silver crucifix and a piece of sacred wafer.

Arriving at Carfax, we went straight into the underground chapel. There, everything was covered with dust. A terrible odour of blood and decay annoyed us. "First, let us make sure how many boxes are here," said the Professor. There were only twenty-nine out of the fifty boxes that the Count had brought to England.

While checking the boxes, we noticed hundreds of red points were glittering in the darkness — rats' eyes! Quincy blew his whistle and his dogs ran into the chapel. They seemed a little afraid at the beginning, but at Quincy's command they attacked and killed some of the rats. The rest of the rats went away into the darkness.

When we came back, I found Mina sleeping. She looked awfully tired.

Tomorrow, we start looking for the missing twenty-one boxes. We have already found a man who said that he had taken nine boxes to an old house in Piccadilly.

Dr Seward's diary
October 3rd

I need to write down what happened to Renfield. I should have paid more attention to him.

We had been discussing the Count's hiding places when we heard a scream. An attendant

19 世紀末のピカデリー・サーカス

rushed to Renfield's room and found him lying on the floor covered with blood. When we reached there, Renfield looked dead. But he suddenly opened his eyes and said, "I had a terrible dream. What's wrong with my face? What is all this blood?"

"Tell us your dream," said the Professor very soothingly.

"I mustn't tell a lie. It was not a dream. It was real. The Count came up to my window in the form of a mist, as he had done many times. I didn't invite him in at first. Then he began to whisper, 'Rats and rats, hundreds of rats. Thousands and millions. Cats will eat them and then all the lives are yours. Come to the window. I will give all these lives to you if you worship me.' I opened the window and said, 'Come in, Master.' He became solid in front of my eyes."

Renfield's voice was getting weaker but he struggled to continue. "Last night Master came again but did not give me anything he had promised. I got angry, but I couldn't stop him from coming in, for Mrs. Harker was in my room and let him in."

We were now alerted and gathered closer to Renfield to listen to him. "When she came to my room this afternoon, she was not the same woman. She was pale. I like women with lots of blood in their veins. But I'm sure Master has taken

all her blood. Tonight, he came again, you know. I tried to stop him, but he threw me down on the floor. I saw him leaving this room in the red mist into the corridor." Renfield heaved a gush of blood and died.

Mina in a peril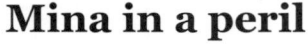

Dr Seward's diary (continued)

The Professor had already dashed to Mrs. Harker's room and we followed him. But the door was locked, so we broke in. The moonlight lit Jonathan Harker lying on the floor almost unconscious. And Mina Harker was…she was kneeling on the bed facing the other direction. In front of her, was the Count facing us. He was pushing her face to his chest. To be more exact, he was forcing her to drink the blood coming out of the scar he himself had made

on his chest. I could see the mark on his forehead that Jonathan had made with the shovel.

His eyes were filled with evil passion. Van Helsing walked towards the Count holding a sacred wafer. We were following the Professor with the silver crucifixes in our hands. The moment the Professor reached the bed, a cloud hid the moon. When the moonlight came back a few seconds later, the Count was gone.

Suddenly Mina Harker began screaming. The hysteric and grieving sounds still echo in my brain. I will never forget it. Her chin was covered with blood.

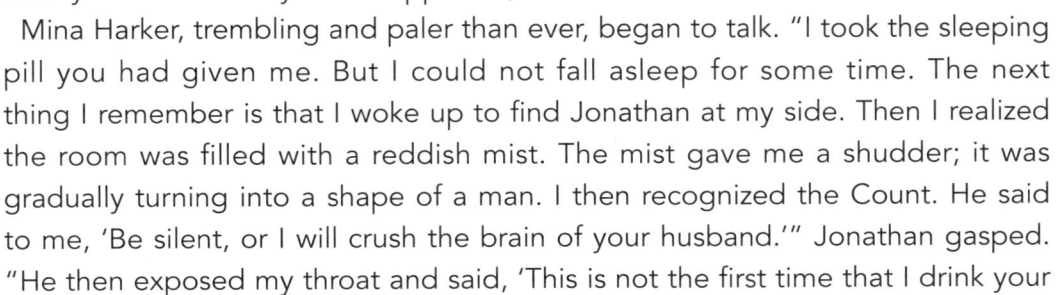

Her scream woke Jonathan. He saw his wife's bloody face and cried, "Mina, dear Mina. In God's name, what does this mean?" The Professor asked her calmly. "Tell us exactly what happened, Mrs. Harker."

Mina Harker, trembling and paler than ever, began to talk. "I took the sleeping pill you had given me. But I could not fall asleep for some time. The next thing I remember is that I woke up to find Jonathan at my side. Then I realized the room was filled with a reddish mist. The mist gave me a shudder; it was gradually turning into a shape of a man. I then recognized the Count. He said to me, 'Be silent, or I will crush the brain of your husband.'" Jonathan gasped. "He then exposed my throat and said, 'This is not the first time that I drink your blood.'" Jonathan groaned. "He said, 'From now on, when my brain orders you to come, you come to me across land or sea.' And he cut his chest with his fingernail, pushed me to it."

I 1〜3とa)〜c)を組み合わせて3つの文を完成しなさい。

1 It was Renfield who revealed
2 The Count's eyes showed evil passion
3 Jonathan gasped and groaned
   a) when he was forcing Mina to drink his blood.
   b) while listening to Mina.
   c) that the Count was with Mina.

II 話の筋に沿ってa)〜e)を並べ替えなさい。

a) The men and the Professor went into the Carfax chapel and found twenty-nine boxes.
b) Mina told Van Helsing what had happened to herself.
c) The men and the Professor saw that the Count was pushing Mina's head onto his chest.
d) Lots of rats appeared and Quincy's dogs killed some of them.
e) Renfield was found lying on the floor covered with blood.

🦷 *Tips for reading*

前から訳すと分かりやすいwhenの複文
We *had been discussing* the Count's hiding places *when* we *heard* a scream.
（伯爵の隠れ家の話をしていたら叫び声が聞こえた。）
Arthur *was about to kiss* Lucy *when* the Professor *pushed* him away.
（アーサーがルーシーにキスをしようとしたところ教授が彼を押しのけた。）

■次の英文を完成しましょう。
I [　　　　　　　　] in bed unable to fall asleep for some time [　] a fog started coming into the room.
（しばらく眠れずにベッドにいたら部屋に霧が入ってきだしたの。）

命令形＋, or　「〜しろ、さもなくば」
Be silent, or I will crush the brain of your husband.
（静かにしろ、さもなければお前の夫の頭を潰すぞ。）

■次の英文を完成しましょう。
Let me in, [　　] I [　　　　　] give you the rats I promised.
（中に入れろ、さもなければ約束のドブネズミはやらんぞ。）

独立不定詞の例
To say nothing of Jonathan, we were all shocked to hear Mina.

(ジョナサンは言うに及ばず、…)

To be honest with you, it was real, not a dream. (正直に言うと、…)

■次の英文を完成しましょう。

1) [   ], the Count was wearing my clothes!

(さらにぞっとしたのは、…)

2) [   ], he was forcing her to drink his blood. (より正確に言えば、…)

< 参考：不定詞でない例 > To my surprise, the Professor became angry with Lucy to hear her complain of the garlic flowers. (驚いたことに、…)

IT   *Listening in and acting out!*

英語を聞いて会話を完成し、互いにパートナーを聞き手としてセリフの練習をしましょう。

I   [1   ]. It was not a dream. It was real. The Count came up to my window [2   ], as he had done many times. I didn't invite him in at first. Then he began to whisper, 'Rats and rats, hundreds of rats. [3   ]. Come to the window. I will give all these lives to you [4   ].'

II   Be silent, or I will crush the brain of your husband. [1   ] I drink your blood. From now on, when [2   ], you come to me across land or sea.

原作にチャレンジ (9)

The moonlight was so bright that through the thick yellow blind the room was light enough to see. On the bed beside the window lay Jonathan Harker, his face flushed, and breathing heavily as though in a stupor. Kneeling on the near edge of the bed facing outwards was the white-clad figure of his wife. By her side stood a tall, thin man, clad in black. His face was turned from us, but the instant we saw it we all recognised the Count—in every way, even to the scar on his forehead. With his left hand, he held both Mrs. Harker's hands, keeping them away with her arms at full tension; his right hand gripped her by the back of the neck, forcing her head down on his bosom. Her white nightdress was smeared with blood, and a thin stream trickled down the man's bare breast which was shown by his torn-open dress. The attitude of the two had a terrible resemblance to a child forcing a kitten's nose into a saucer of milk to compel it to drink.

コラム3 「血まみれの尼僧」から「女吸血鬼たち」、そして「ドラキュラ」へ

ブラム・ストーカーの『ドラキュラ』(1897) は、恐怖小説の一つの完成形とされる。そして、「小説」と今われわれが呼ぶ読み物は 250 年ほど前のイギリスで登場した。孤島に漂流した男のサバイバル日誌『ロビンソン・クルーソー』(1719) や、若い住み込み女中が両親に宛てた手紙という体裁の『パメラ』(1740) あたりがその始まりだとされる。これらはまさに『ドラキュラ』の、手紙や日記や新聞記事でリアリティを演出する手法につながっている。

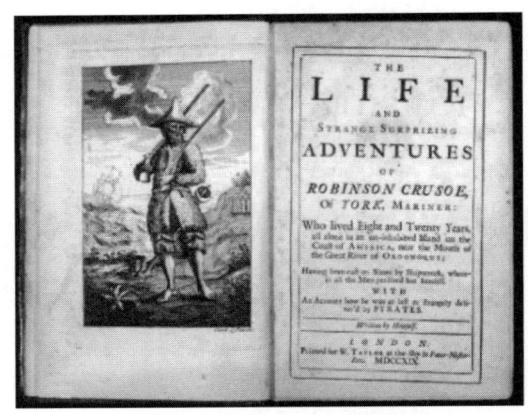

『ロビンソン・クルーソー』初版

18 世紀のイギリスで小説の登場を見た背景には、中層の人々の経済力と識字率の上昇、定期刊行物の普及や逸早い読者層の形成といった、相互に関係する要素があった。そして、あからさまな絵空事を避けて事実の報告という形をとったのは、読者にも書き手にも質実をよしとする風潮があったからだろう。たとえば『ロビンソン・クルーソー』の作者デフォーの手になるとされる「ヴィール夫人の幽霊」(1706) は、物語というよりもむしろ幽霊との遭遇の「事実報告」であり、フィクションなのかジャーナリストの先駆者たるデフォーの書いた記事なのか判断が分かれる。

ウォルポールの屋敷内部

恐怖小説の嚆矢とされるのは世紀半ばに出た『オトラント城奇譚』(1764) であるが、これは必ずしも商人や奉公人といった読者層に向けたものではなかった。どこからか巨大な甲冑の部分が徐々に現れ、巨人が完成して悪党による城の乗っ取りを阻止する、という短編で、古代ギリシャ悲劇に見る予言の実現のような構造を持つ「悪夢」と評される。作者は時の首相の息子ホレス・ウォルポールで、ゴシック風の屋敷を建てて流行の奔りとするなど、独自の趣味の世界を追究した人だった。『オトラント城奇譚』の前書きにも趣味人らしく、信ぴょう性を特徴とする小説に「荒唐無稽」な絵空事を取り込む実験的試みである、と記している。

しかしながらこのあと 18 世紀後半、小説が娯楽として浸透するにつれ、庶民に人気を博する「恐怖もの」が次々と出版されていく。書籍は 19 世紀に廉価本が普及するまで非常に高価だったため、読者の多くは馬車で移動する貸本屋（巡回図書館）を利用していたのだが、18 世紀末はその品ぞろえの 9 割を恐怖小説が占めていたのである。なぜ、

「血まみれの尼僧」の挿絵

こんなふうに数十年で恐怖ものが読み物の主流に踊り出たのだろう。

　有力なのは、虚構の恐怖をひととき堪能することによって、逆に安定した社会の一員としての自己の安寧を確認しようとする心性があった、という説である。大陸ヨーロッパの国々が市民革命の嵐にもまれるなか、確かにイギリスは、18 世紀を通して相対的な平和を享受し、安定した暮らしは徐々に裾野を広げていった。

　では 18 世紀後半、イギリス人はどんな恐怖を堪能して己が安寧をかみしめたのだろう。

　初期の恐怖ものは、中世の建物を舞台とする小説以前のお話、という意味で「ゴシック物語 (Gothic tales)」と呼ばれる。（ロマネスク教会も要塞建築もイングランドの一般読者にとって中世は「ゴシック」だったのである。）ゴシック物語に頻繁に登場したのはフランスやイタリアの尼僧や修道僧、そして貴族たちで、彼らは修道院や古城を舞台に淫欲や残虐行為にふける姿で描かれた。なかでも血に染まった白い衣装（多くは花嫁衣裳）で主人公を襲う「血まみれの尼僧 (bleeding nun)」は、定番キャラクターとして繰り返し登場した。

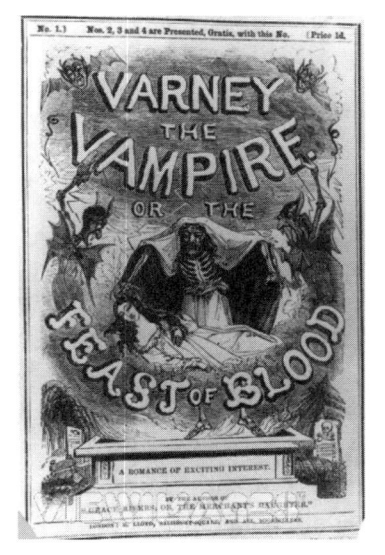

『吸血鬼バーニー』表紙

　さて 18 世紀末から 19 世紀になると、舞台はイギリスや今のアイルランド、つまり読者の身近なところとなり、「血まみれの尼僧」に代表される恐ろしい女性キャラクターに同時代性が与えられる。死んで物の怪となり夜な夜な男の夢枕に立ちその精を奪う女、また亡霊となって不道徳な行いを娘たちに教える貴婦人、夢遊病でさまよう謎の美女などヴァリエーション豊かに発展するのである。そして次の時代、それが「女吸血鬼もの」に昇華されていく。

　吸血鬼伝説は古くから各地にあり、1819 年には『吸血鬼』というタイトルのマイナーな作品が出ているし、またジョン・ポリドリという医者の書いた『吸血鬼バーニー』(1847) は、メアリー・シェリーが『フランケンシュタイン』を書いたとき、いっしょにスイス湖畔の古城にこもって即興的に書いた話として知られている。初の本格的吸血鬼小説と呼べるのは『吸血鬼カーミラ』で、これはブラム・ストーカーがコラムを書いていた雑誌の主宰者シェリダン・レ・ファニュの作である。生前は欲

『吸血鬼カーミラ』表紙

望の赴くまま生きたウィステリア伯爵夫人カーミラが、死後、イギリスの娘たちを次々と襲って「レズビアニズム」を伝導していく、という話だ。

こうして「血まみれの尼僧」からカーミラまでをふりかえると、「血」「夢遊病」「同性を悪に誘う」「男の精を奪う」など、女吸血鬼たちの原型は1897年の『ドラキュラ』発表までにすでに準備されており、観客や読者の受け入れ態勢もできていたと推測できる。

そして、イギリス近代に育まれたこの伝統的な恐怖は、作者ストーカーの無意識にも沈殿していたようである。ロンドンのショービジネス界で充実した日々をおくるかたわら、『ドラキュラ』執筆までの数年間、実は繰り返し同じ夢に悩まされていた、という。「官能的な女が3人、どこからともなく立ち現れて自分のベッドに迫ってくる。女たちは唇を求めることなく、自分の首元に恐ろしい形相でむしゃぶりつく。自分は恐怖と恍惚の入りまじった感触を生々しく残して目が覚める」と書き残している。これはまさに『ドラキュラ』に登場する3人の女吸血鬼の描写ではないだろうか。ウォルポールの荒唐無稽な夢物語から始まった恐怖小説は、ストーカーによって迫力と心理的リアリティを備えた「男の恐怖」の物語に到達したのである。

では、イギリス小説の歴史において恐怖の経糸を担った彼女らは、いったいどういう存在だったのだろう。

たとえば「牡丹灯篭」や「四谷怪談」、あるいは『雨月物語』の女たちのように、わが国にも定番の女の幽霊や魔物がいるが、彼女らは一様に、特定の男への恨みや執着からおぞましい行いに及ぶ、怖いがどこか哀れで美しい存在である。一方、イギリス恐怖小説の女たちは、ひたすらに強烈な嫌悪を引き起こす存在だった。「イタリアやフランスの古城や修道院の貴族や修道僧、ことに貴婦人や尼僧」という設定から推察できることだが、その嫌悪の背後には、政党政治が安定して市民的価値観が定着するなかイギリス国民が感じた、大陸の絶対王制やカソリック教会の支配に対する侮蔑や敵意があった。18世紀には、男女ともがレースや化粧や香水を身に着けたフランス風モードの流行や、フランス貴婦人のサロンなどをこぞって真似する自国の上流に対する反感があったかもしれない。また19世紀、一足早く産業が発展するなか、前の時代まで文化的にカトリック国に後塵を拝していた自国の文化的な優位性を主張しようとする機運があり、それも関係していると思われる。女吸血鬼は、一流国となったイギリス国民が嫌悪し、克服し、侮蔑して優越感を感じるべき対象の象徴だったと言えるだろう。

ところで、演劇批評家を経て劇場の仕事についていた『ドラキュラ』の作者ストーカーは、じつは最初から舞台にのせることを意識して小説『ドラキュラ』を書いていた。そして「活劇」としてヒットさせるため、主役を女でなく、ゴシック小説で神出鬼没にアクションを担ってきた「悪党 (villain)」に設定した。この場合の「悪党」とは、イタリアやフランスの残虐な僧や貴族のことある。登場人物が力を合わせて悪党を退治する舞台のフィナーレでは、観客はイギリス社会が魔手から守られたことに安堵し、心を一つにして拍手喝采するはずである。とはいえ、地下鉄が通りガス灯が夜道を照らす時代に古くさいキャラクターを主役にして受けるはずはない。それに、大革命からコミューンを経て市民社会への変貌を遂げたフランスや、統一運動で近代国家の形を整えつつあ

ったイタリアは、もはや過去の非文明を体現する場所ではない。そこで、思い切ってもっと東へ、もっと異世界へ…。やはりかねてから資料を集めていた東欧の戦国君主ヴラド・ドラクル（コラム2参照）こそが、「科学と文明の市民社会」から見た究極の「他者」であり、尼僧や女吸血鬼が体現してきた非文明を象徴的に引き継ぐ存在なのである。ドラキュラ伯爵の領国トランシルヴァニア (Transilvania) は、じっさいはヴラド3世の国ワラキアの隣国だったが、その名は「森を (sylvia) 超えた (trans) 場所」を意味し、カルパチア山脈の秘境、文明の向こう側を連想させることから、ここをドラキュラ城の地と設定したと思われる。

　教会支配や絶対王制の過去、異文化、非科学と非文明、女の支配や堕落と欲望への恐れ…。これらが混然と成す土壌から立ちのぼる恐怖の具現、それがドラキュラなのである。

参考資料：NHK『知への旅』シリーズ「イギリスの恐怖文学2」（NHK1997年放映、BBC1994年放映）
　　　　Horror Fiction in the Protestant Tradition (Victor Sage, MacMillan ,1988)
　　　　『身体で読むファンタジー』第Ⅱ部「モンストラス・フェミニン」（吉田純子編、人文書院、2004）他

Chapter 10

ミナ、「探知機」となる

👤 *Get ready!*

授業に臨む準備をしましょう。

I 日本語と英語を一致させなさい。

1 厳粛な　　2 滅びる　　3 沈んだようすで　　4 紙幣　　5 復讐

6 絶望的に　　7 遠い　　8 落ち着いた　　9 現象　　10 恍惚状態

desperately　　solemn　　sedated　　banknotes　　revenge

phenomenon　　trance　　remote　　perish　　despondently

II 次の語句を辞書で調べましょう。

hypnotize（名詞 hypnosis）　　mission　　flinch　　outcast

detector　　baptism　　ominous　　misery

⚰️ *Enjoy the story!*

予習のための質問です。答えの参照となる英文部分を特定し、答えを日本語で準備しておきましょう。

1 What happened when Van Helsing touched Mina's forehead with a piece of sacred wafer?
　ヴァン・ヘルシングがミナの額を聖餅で触れるとどうなったか。

2 What did Count Dracula say when he landed on the paved yard?
　舗装地に着地してドラキュラ伯爵は何と言ったか。

3 Why did Van Helsing say that Count Dracula was afraid of the men and in a hurry?
　ドラキュラ伯爵は自分たちを恐れ、かつ急いでいるとヴァン・ヘルシングが言うのはなぜか。

4 What struck Jonathan's mind?
　何がジョナサンの心を打ったのか。

5 What was Van Helsing's explanation of the "remarkable phenomenon" shown by Mina?
　ミナが見せた「注目すべき現象」についてヴァン・ヘルシングはどんな説明をしたか。

Cornering the Count

Jonathan Harker's diary
October 3rd

We discussed our plans again. We decided to first sterilize the twenty-nine boxes placed in the chapel of Carfax before pursuing the Count to Piccadilly. The Professor said, "We have to be prepared for the most horrible and dangerous mission that each one of us has ever experienced. Here, we now make a solemn pact that we will never give up and continue our fight till the monster perishes."

He then said to Mina, "You will be safe while we are out. I have put garlic flowers and crucifixes in your room so that the Count cannot come in." Saying this, he touched her forehead with a piece of sacred wafer. She screamed. It had burnt her forehead like a piece of hot metal. She flinched. And she murmured despondently, "I'm unclean." Then she cried, "Unclean! God will refuse me if I die now." "God will remove this mark from your forehead. Perhaps we are the instruments of God," said the Professor.

After a few seconds, Mina raised her head and replied in a low but firm voice, "I am ready for anything." Her words filled us with courage.

We hurried to Carfax and sterilized the boxes in the chapel. Then we went on to the Piccadilly house. But we found only eight of the nine boxes we had expected to find there. However, we found some documents and keys with labels. Some of the labels had the addresses of the Count's other houses in London. There were also several kinds of foreign banknotes and gold coins on the floor. The monster must have been in a hurry. "He is afraid of us," said the Professor.

Arthur and Quincy went to the addresses shown on the labels.

While waiting for their return, we received a message from Mina delivered by an asylum attendant. It said, "It is 12:45 now and the Count is going to the Piccadilly house." The Professor exclaimed, "He is coming here." We soon heard the knock at the door. It was Arthur and Quincy. "We have sterilized

twelve boxes," reported Arthur. Thus, there was only one box missing.

Then we heard quiet footsteps on the staircase. And the next moment, the Count had leapt into the room. Jonathan, standing in front of the door lest the Count should flee, tried to stab him with a knife. But the Count was quicker. He picked up the foreign banknotes and jumped out of the window breaking the panes.

Landing on the paved yard, he turned to us and said, "My revenge has just started. I can live forever. Time is on my side. The women you love are mine already! You too will be mine with their help!"
He disappeared into the crowd.

After a minute of silence, the Professor said, "We have learned much. He is afraid of us and wants to leave England. That's why he desperately needed the foreign banknotes."

Mina, the detector

2-9

Jonathan Harker's diary (continued)

When we went back to the asylum, we told Mina everything. I tried to be cheerful. But it was painful to see the red mark on her forehead. Probably seeing through me, Mina said to me, "Jonathan, I want you to remember something. I know you must destroy the Count as you did Lucy. And me, too, if it should become necessary. But you cannot do this with hate. The Count, who caused all this misery, is the saddest case. But when the evil part of him perishes, the good part will be with God." I was struck by her words. Though she now looks an outcast with the ominous mark, she is the nearest to God.

Jonathan Harker's diary
October 4th

This morning, Mina woke me just before dawn. She told me to bring the Professor to her immediately. "I want to see him now. I think I can be useful."
"How?" I asked. "He must put me under hypnosis. I may be able to report what the Count is doing."

When the Professor came to our room, she repeated these words to him. He told her to sit and began hypnotizing her right away. In a few minutes, her eyes were closed, but half-opened after a while and she started to respond in

a remote, sedated voice which was unfamiliar to me.

"Where are you?"

"I don't know."

"What do you see?"

"Nothing. I'm in the darkness."

"What do you hear?"

"The sound of water, outside."

"What else?"

"I can hear some men walking above me."

"What are you doing?"

"Nothing. I'm still. Still like death."

Then Mina closed her eyes and started to make a soft sound of breathing. She had fallen asleep. The sun had risen. I asked the Professor what was going on. He explained a most remarkable phenomenon.

"The Count forced your wife to drink his blood. It was, so to speak, the Count's baptism of blood, and he won control over her mind. But at dawn and sunset, when his control becomes weak, I can hypnotize her. While she is under hypnosis, she half regains her reasonable self but half remains in a trance. She thus can read the Count's mind." The Professor continued. "Now we know he is escaping by sea in the box filled with decayed earth. He is most probably heading for his castle in Transylvania."

I 1〜3とa) 〜c) を組み合わせて3つの文を完成しなさい。

　1 Van Helsing touched Mina's forehead with a piece of sacred wafer,
　2 The labels on the keys left in the Piccadilly house
　3 When the Professor put Mina under hypnosis,
　　a) which left an ominous mark on the spot.
　　b) she could read the Count's mind.
　　c) carried the addresses of the Count's other houses in London.

II 話の筋に沿って a) 〜 e) を並べ替えなさい。

　a) The Professor and the men went to Carfax to sterilize the boxes.
　b) Mina, put under hypnosis, revealed that the Count was being transported by sea.
　c) Arthur and Quincy went to the other houses of the Count.
　d) The Count came back to the Piccadilly house to get the foreign banknotes he desperately needed.
　e) The Professor and the men went to the house in Piccadilly and found some keys.

🦷 *Tips for reading*

If 主語 should … 「万が一…なら」「たとえ…となるようなことがあっても」
I know you will have to destroy me *if it should become necessary*.
（万が一そうすることが必要になれば、あなたは私を殺さねばならないって分かってます。）

■次の英文を完成しましょう。
　What would happen [　　　　　　　　　] fail to destroy the monster?
　（われわれがあの怪物を退治しそこねるようなことがあったらどうなるのだろう。）

特定の事や物や人の "some--" something あること，someone ある人
I want you to remember *something*. （ひとつあなたに憶えておいて欲しいの。）

■次の英文を完成しましょう。
　R: "Master! Where are you going?"
　D: "I have come here to see [　　　　　　], not you."
　（「ご主人様。いずこへ。」「ここへは、お前ではなく、ある者に会いに来たのだ。」）

英語を聞いて会話を完成し、パートナーと互いにモノローグの練習をしましょう。

I [1   ]. I can live forever. [2   ]. The women you love are mine already! You too will be mine with their help!

II Jonathan, I want you to remember something. I know you must destroy the Count as you did Lucy. And me, too, [1   ]. But you cannot do this with hate. The Count, [2   ], is the saddest case. When the evil part of him perishes, however, [3   ].

原作にチャレンジ (10)

The next instant, with a sinuous dive he swept under Harker's arm ere his blow could fall, and, grasping a handful of the money from the floor, dashed across the room, and threw himself at the window. Amid the crash and glitter of the falling glass, he tumbled into the flagged area below. Through the sound of the shivering glass I could hear the "ting" of the gold, as some of the sovereigns fell on the flagging.

We ran over and saw him spring unhurt from the ground. He, rushing up the steps, crossed the flagged yard, and pushed open the stable door. There he turned and spoke to us:

"You think to baffle me, you—with your pale faces all in a row, like sheep in a butcher's. You shall be sorry yet, each one of you! You think you have left me without a place to rest; but I have more. My revenge is just begun! I spread it over centuries, and time is on my side. Your girls that you all love are mine already; and through them you and others shall yet be mine—my creatures, to do my bidding and to be my jackals when I want to feed. Bah!"

Chapter 11

再び、トランシルヴァニアへ

👤 *Get ready!*

授業に臨む準備をしましょう。

I 日本語と英語を一致させてください。

　1 心待ちにしている　　2 試練　　3 巧みに　　4 追跡する　　5 抵抗する
　6 不安　　7 棺台　　8 刻む　　9 おぞましい　　10 待ち伏せる

engrave　　anxious　　ordeal　　ghastly　　ambush
cunningly　　catafalque　　pursue　　resist　　anxiety

II Google Map で次の場所を確認しておきましょう。

　1 the Black Sea　　　2 Varna in Bulgaria
　3 the Dardanelles　　4 Galatz and Veresti in Rumania

⚰ *Enjoy the story!*

予習のための質問です。答えの参照となる英文部分を特定し、答えを日本語で準備しておきましょう。

1 How did Count Dracula trick his enemies?
　ドラキュラ伯爵は、どのように敵を欺いたか。

2 What happened to the Czarina Catharine, according to its captain?
　船長によると、ツァリーナ・キャサリン（女帝エカテリーナ）号に何がおこったのか。

3 What appeared from the darkness to Van Helsing and Mina at about midnight.?
　真夜中ごろ、ヴァン・ヘルシングとミナのもとに何が現れたか。

4 What happened to Van Helsing when he could not move in front of the coffin of a female vampire?
　女吸血鬼の棺の前で動けなくなっていたヴァン・ヘルシングに何がおこったか。

5 What did Van Helsing do to Count Dracula's coffin?
　ヴァン・ヘルシングはドラキュラ伯爵の棺に何をしたか。

To Transylvania

Mina Harker's diary
October 5th, 5 p.m.

It was not difficult to find the ship that took the Count onto the route back to Transylvania, because there was only one ship going to the Black Sea—the Czarina Catherine bound for the port of Varna.

The old route of the Oriental Express

I'm going with the others this time. I have no idea what I would be like when I am in the Count's territory. However, I'm anxious to see the place where my husband had that terrible ordeal.

Dr Seward's diary
October 28th

The Count has cunningly tricked us!

On the 12th, we left Charing Cross in the morning and arrived in Paris at night. There we took the Orient Express and travelled night and day, and finally, on the 15th, arrived here in Varna, a port town on the Black Sea. We then

received news that the Czarina Catherine was sailing through the Dardanelles as we had expected. But today, we received another telegram, which told us that the ship had entered the port of Galatz, further north on the Black Sea from Varna.

Mina Harker's diary
October 30th

On arriving at the port of Galatz, we went to see the captain of the Czarina Catherine. He said that the ship had been surrounded by a dense fog during most of the voyage and that it had travelled unusually fast. When the fog was cleared, the captain could see the surroundings; the ship was already near Galatz instead of Varna.

Soon we found that a man named Skinksy had taken the box containing the Count at the Galatz port and that this Skinksy had been found dead later. We also came to know that before his death, he had given the box to some Slovaks. When I was hypnotized this evening, I could hear little waves. It is evident that the Count is moving on the river. The river that flows closest to his castle is the Sereth. The Count cannot cross running water on his own, so this is an opportunity we should not miss. We must do our best to catch him on the river of Sereth.

We have decided to pursue him in three groups taking two different routes. I'm going to Veresti with the Professor by train and buy a carriage with horses at the station to reach the castle. Arthur and Jonathan will try to catch up with the Count's boat on the water. Quincy and Dr Seward will follow them on horses on the riverbank. Each of us has a gun and a knife, for the Slovaks will resist us.

To the Castle

Mina Harker's diary
November 2nd

The scenery is getting wilder as we are getting closer to the Carpathians. By tomorrow morning we will reach the spot on the Borgo Pass where my husband met the Count.

Van Helsing's diary
November 5th, early morning

Yesterday, at around sunset, as we were driving the carriage, the Count's castle showed itself. It looked exactly like what Jonathan Harker had described in his diary. I felt anxiety but also thrilled.

We stopped the carriage near the castle and prepared a fire and some food. Although Mina was shaking, she did not eat anything. I drew a circle with some pieces of sacred wafer around us. Mina and I stayed in it. The mark on Mina's forehead seemed to glow as the sun set below the mountains.

At about midnight, from the

darkness around us, three female vampires appeared. They seemed freely floating in the air but did not come into the circle. "Come, Sister, come," they invited Mina. At dawn, they finally disappeared.

November 5th, afternoon

Mina was sleeping in the circle. I left her and went to the chapel of the castle. I knew where it was from Jonathan's diary. I had to find the graves of the three women. I looked and looked and found one at last.

One of the women was sleeping in the coffin. She was full of life. I almost felt it wrong to drive a stake into her body. I had been unable to move for a while, when I heard Mina calling to me, or rather to my mind. At her call, I woke up from the trance. In fact, it was impossible to hear her voice in the chapel. I think she somehow saved me by working on my mind. Then I did what I had to do. I found two more coffins near the first one and pushed myself to do the same. I'm glad I did not wait hesitating till dark.

Then, I found a tomb of a bigger size. In the tomb, a coffin was placed on a stone catafalque, on which was engraved the name:

Dracula

The coffin was empty. I placed a piece of sacred wafer in it.

As soon as I returned into the circle to join Mina, she said, "Let us leave this ghastly place and join the others! They are coming here soon." Mina and I decided to ambush the Count carried on the wagon.

Ⅰ 1〜3と a)〜c) を組み合わせて 3 つの文を完成しなさい。

1 When the Professor saw the castle,
2 Mina was shaking in the circle
3 Mina called to the mind of the Professor,

   a) he felt thrilled as well as afraid.
   b) which woke him up from a trance.
   c) but did not eat anything.

Ⅱ 話の筋に沿って a)〜e) を並べ替えなさい。

   a) The Professor made a circle using sacred wafer and left Mina in it.
   b) The Professor went to the chapel of the castle and drove stakes into the bodies of the female vampires.
   c) Mina reached the Borgo Pass with the Professor.
   d) The news reached Dr Seward that the Czarina Catherine had sailed to Galatz instead of Varna.
   e) The Professor, Mina, and the others took the Orient Express from Charing Cross in London to Paris.

🧛 *Tips for reading*

be anxious to- 不定詞　〜するのが待ちきれない
I'm anxious to see the place where my husband had that terrible ordeal.
（夫があの恐ろしい試練を受けた場所を見るのが待ちきれない。）

■次の英文を完成しましょう。

The Count was [   ] England; he was afraid of Van Helsing.（伯爵はイングランドを去るのが待ちきれなかった。ヴァン・ヘルシングを恐れたのである。）

＜参考＞ Lucy in the coffin, in fact, might have been anxious for a peaceful death.
（棺の中のルーシーは、実のところ、静かな死を切望していたのかもしれない。）

on 〜 ing (=the moment 〜 / as soon as 〜)　〜するやいなや
On arriving at the port of Galatz, we went to see the captain.
(=As soon as we arrived at the port of Galatz, ….)
The moment Arthur stepped forward to her, she jumped to him.
(=On Arthur('s) stepping forward to her, she….)

■ as soon as または the moment を使って次の英文を書き直しましょう。

   1) On receiving the second telegram, Seward realized he had been tricked.

■ on -ing　を使って次の英文を書き直しましょう。（註：〜 ing の主語は、代名詞の場合、所有格となる）

2) The moment they raised the rifles, the Slovaks pulled out their knives.

3) As soon as I returned into the circle, Mina said, "Let's join the others."

ⅠⅠ *Listening in and acting out!*

英語を聞いて会話を完成し、パートナーと口頭練習をしましょう。

A: What happened to your ship, Captain?

B: Well, the ship was [1   ] during most of the voyage, but somehow it travelled unusually fast.

A: Then what?

B: [2   ], I found my ship was near Galatz, instead of Varna.

A: [3   ] loaded on your ship?

B: A man named Skinksy took them at the Galatz port. He had the documents from the sender with him all right.

A: [4   ] with the box?

B: Well, he said he was going to hand it over to some Slovaks.

原作にチャレンジ（11）

This then was the Un-Dead home of the King-Vampire, to whom so many more were due. Its emptiness spoke eloquent to make certain what I knew. Before I began to restore these women to their dead selves through my awful work, I laid in Dracula's tomb some of the Wafer, and so banished him from it, Un-Dead, forever.

Then I began my terrible task, and I dreaded it. Had it been but one, it had been easy, comparative. But three! To begin twice more after I had been through a deed of horror; for if it was terrible with the sweet Miss Lucy, what would it not be with these strange ones who had survived through centuries, and who had been strengthened by the passing of the years; who would, if they could, have fought for their foul lives....

Chapter 12

終焉

Get ready!

授業に臨む準備をしましょう。日本語と英語を一致させてください。

1 小さな尖塔　　2 洞穴　　3 双眼鏡　　4 永遠　　5 停まる
6 鞭打つ　　7 あちこちに散る　　8 （言葉などを）発する
9 息を引き取る　　10 廃墟

flog　　halt　　disperse　　cave　　eternity
binoculars　　expire　　ruin　　utter　　pinnacle

Enjoy the story!

予習のための質問です。答えの参照となる英文部分を特定し、答えを日本語で準備しておきましょう。

1 What did Mina see after Van Hensling had cried "Look!" for the second time?
ヴァン・ヘルシングが再度「見なさい！」と叫んだあとミナは何を見たか。

2 What did Jonathan, Arthur, Quincy, and Seward do as soon as the Slovaks stopped the wagon?
スロヴァキア人が馬車を停めるとすぐ、ジョナサンとアーサー、そしてクィンシーとセワードは何をしたか。

3 What did the Count's face look like when Jonathan removed the lid of the box?
ジョナサンが箱の蓋を外したとき、伯爵はどんな表情をしていたか。

4 What happened to Count Dracula when Quincy stabbed him? And what change did Quincy notice on Mina's face?
クィンシーがドラキュラ伯爵を刺したとき、伯爵はどうなったか。クィンシーはミナの顔のどんな変化に気づいたか。

5 What was the Castle of Dracula like when the Harker family revisited it?
ハーカー一家がドラキュラ城を再訪したとき、城はどんなようすだったか。

The last battle

Mina Harker's diary

November 6th

Early in the evening, Professor Van Helsing and I started walking eastward to join Jonathan and the others. Carrying heavy blankets and some food, we could move only slowly. But I knew from which direction they were coming on the winding road. We looked back at the castle. It was standing on the high precipice with some pointed pinnacles. The silhouette against the orange-grey sky was beautiful but terrifying.

Then we heard some wolves howling. Though the howling was in the distance, we decided to find a protected spot in case they should come near us. Soon the Professor found a little cave in a giant rock. "Mrs. Harker. Rest in here. You'll be safe and less cold." He then climbed the giant rock and stood on it with a pair of binoculars in his hands. I followed him instead of resting in the cave. He looked out for the horses of his friends.

The Professor cried out, "Look!" and handed the binoculars to me. The wind mixed with powder snow was blowing but I could see a large wagon. It was carrying a long square box on it. And some men on horses were escorting the wagon. "This is going to be the end of the Count. Otherwise, …. We should take actions

before the Count becomes free." As I said this to myself I could hear my heart beating. The sunset was near.

The End

Mina Harker's diary (continued)

The Professor jumped down and drew a big circle around the rock using some pieces of sacred wafer. Then, as he looked up, he shouted again. "Look!" I could see two men flogging their horses were after the wagon. They were getting closer to it. We waited for the wagon and the horses to come nearer. Every moment seemed like an eternity because I knew the sun would go down in some minutes.

A man shouted, "Halt!" It was my Jonathan. The Slovaks escorting the wagon probably understood the sharp tone of the voice, for they stopped their horses. At the same time, Arthur and Jonathan were on one side of the wagon. Quincy and Dr Seward were on the other. The leader of the Slovaks gave an order to move on, but the four men raised their Winchester rifles. The Professor below the rock and I on top of it also raised our rifles.

The Slovaks stopped, and at another command of the leader they pulled out their knives and pistols. Jonathan and Quincy jumped up onto the wagon and pushed the men away from it. Jonathan, with an incredible strength, raised the box and threw it on the ground. He and Quincy jumped down from the wagon and raced to the box.

But I saw Quincy was holding his side, from which blood was coming out.

カルパチア山脈の日没

He continued helping Jonathan to pull off the lid from the box. The Count was lying on the earth in it. His eyes were glittering with the horrible anger which I knew too well. The sun was almost touching the top of the mountain. I could tell the Count was watching the setting sun.

In an instant, however, Jonathan's knife flashed. It cut through the Count's throat. At the same time, Quincy's knife went into his heart. The next moment, the Count's body was turning into dust and disappeared.

It was like a miracle. And I can look back at this battle with a feeling of relief, not of tension and terror, because the dim sun light showed me a moment of a look — a look of peace on the face of the perishing Count.

The Slovaks had dispersed in fear. But the saddest moment was waiting for us. Quincy had fallen to the ground with his hand holding against his side. Now blood was flowing out. I jumped down and ran to him. The circle of sacred wafer did not stop me. I held his hand but could not utter a word. I think Quincy saw the sadness in my face. He smiled at me and said, "Don't be sad. I am glad to have saved you. You no longer have the mark on your forehead." Then he expired.

Note to the diary, seven years later written by Jonathan Harker (2-14)

Seven years ago, we had a horrid experience. But Mina and I think that the happiness we have now is worth the suffering. We named our little boy Quincy. This summer, the three of us made a journey to Transylvania. To our surprise, the castle had turned into a real ruin.

I looked for official documents concerning the Count to make a record of what exactly had happened. But most of what is left to us is our personal diaries and letters. Mina said, "We don't need proof. When this boy is grown up, he will know how his brave father with his brave friends risked their own lives and helped his mother."

Ⅰ 1〜3とa)〜c) を組み合わせて3つの文を完成しなさい。

  1 Mina did not go into the cave to rest but

  2 Mina had seen a look of peace on the Count's face

  3 Mina and Jonathan named their son

   a) after the man who had bravely fought the Count and died.

   b) just before he turned into dust.

   c) raised a Winchester rifle on the giant rock.

Ⅱ 話の筋に沿って a)〜e) を並べ替えなさい。

  a) Jonathan and the others caught up with the wagon.

  b) Mina and Van Helsing started walking eastward to join the others.

  c) Van Helsing saw a wagon carrying a large box coming on the road.

  d) Jonathan and Quincy killed the Count.

  e) Hearing wolves howl, Van Helsing looked for a protected spot for Mina.

🦷 **Tips for reading**

現代分詞（-ing）で、理由、時（「ながら」「あとで」「したとき」等）、譲歩、条件・仮定などを表現できる。

理由の分詞構文

Carrying heavy blankets, we could move only slowly.

（重い毛布を携えていたので、われわれはゆっくりとしか動けなかった。）

時の分詞構文

Saying this, Lucy fell asleep （こう言いながらルーシーは眠りに落ちた。）

Landing on the paved yard, he turned to us.

（舗装地に着地するなり奴はこちらを向いた。）

Watching the sunset scenery, I noticed someone was coming out of the window below.

（夕日の景色を見ていたら、誰かが下の窓から出てくるのに気づいた。）

譲歩の分詞構文

Arthur, (being) shocked to see Lucy, was willing to do anything.

（衝撃を受けながらもアーサーは何でもする気だった。）注記：「衝撃を受けたので」と理由に解釈も可。

条件・仮定の分詞構文

Arthur is doing okay *considering his loss*.

（大切な人を亡くしたことを思えば、アーサーは何とかやっている。）

■次の英文を日本語に訳しましょう。
　1) Understanding the tone of Jonathan's voice, the Slovaks stopped.
　2) Probably seeing through me, Mina said that we should not destroy the Count with hate.

先行詞を含む関係代名詞 what
Jonathan tried to find some official record to prove *what* had happened.
(ジョナサンは、起こったことを証明する何か公式の記録を見つけようとした。)

■次の文を日本語に訳しましょう。
　The castle looked exactly like what Jonathan had described in his diary.

■次の英文を完成しましょう。
　[　　　　　　　] Dr Seward told about Renfield [　　　　　　　] Mina.
　(セワード医師がレンフィールドについて言ったことはミナの興味を引いた。)

in case …should ～ =lest …should ～　（～するといけないので / ～した場合にそなえて）
We decided to find a protected spot *in case the wolves should come near us*.
(狼たちが近づいた場合にそなえて守られた場所を見つけることにした。)

■次の英文を日本語に訳しましょう。
　1) The Professor drew a circle around us using sacred wafer in case the female vampires should appear.
　2) Jonathan stood in front of the door lest the Count should flee.

ⅠT　*Listening in and acting out!*

英語を聞いて会話を完成し、パートナーと口頭練習をしましょう。
　A: I wanted to make a record of what exactly had happened. So, I looked for [1　　　　　　　　　　　　　　　　　　　　　].
　B: At the British Library, you mean?
　A: Yes. I couldn't find any, though. It looks like all what is left to us is [2　　　　　　　　　　　　　　　　　].
　B: Well, my dear. After all, we don't need proof. When our boy is grown up, he will know how his father with his friends bravely [3　　　　　　　　　　] to help his mother and England.
　A: Yes. And you were brave, too, Mina. That horrid experience has led to our present happiness. The heart of Quincy [4　　　　　　　　　　　].

Seven years ago, we all went through the flames; and the happiness of some of us since then is, we think, well worth the pain we endured. It is an added joy to Mina and to me that our boy's birthday is the same day as that on which Quincey Morris died. His mother holds, I know, the secret belief that some of our brave friend's spirit has passed into him. His bundle of names links all our little band of men together; but we call him Quincey.

In the summer of this year we made a journey to Transylvania, and went over the old ground which was, and is, to us so full of vivid and terrible memories. It was almost impossible to believe that the things which we had seen with our own eyes and heard with our own ears were living truths. Every trace of all that had been was blotted out. The castle stood as before, reared high above a waste of desolation.

コラム4　映画『ドラキュラ』

『魔人ドラキュラ』DVD 輸入盤

ストーカーの『ドラキュラ』は数多くの映像作品の源泉となってきた。なかでも彼の小説を大筋忠実に映像化して広く知られるのは3作で、まずハリウッドのトッド・ブラウニング監督『魔人ドラキュラ』（原題 *Dracula*）である。無声映画を脱し「トーキー」となったばかりの1931年に上映された。ドラキュラがミナを連れ去ったりレンフィールドが脱走したり、筋書きは原作と若干異なるものの、映像、脚本とも質が高く今も楽しめる。

主演のルゴシ・ベーラ（本名ブラシュコー・ベーラ・フェレンツ・デジェ, 1882-1956）はオーストリア＝ハンガリー二重帝国のハンガリー、つまりまさにかつてのトランシルヴァニアで生まれ、20代で国民劇場の舞台に立った。第一次世界大戦が勃発したとき有名俳優として兵役を免除されていたが、愛国心から志願し従軍している。

終戦直後1919年、俳優の労働組合を組織するも、すぐに革命政権が崩壊し、亡命を余儀なくされる。まずベルリンに行くが、1921年、船員としてアメリカに移住をした。

1926年、ニューヨークで仲間とともに母国語で上演するハンガリー劇場を立ち上げると、翌1927年、才能を見出され、アイルランド出身のハミルトン・ディーンらの制作によってブルトン劇場で英語上演されていた『ドラキュラ』に出演するようになる。

そしてこのころハリウッドで、この舞台をもとにした映

画製作の計画が進んでいたが、当初主演はルゴシ・ベーラの予定ではなかった。しかし1929年に大恐慌が起こって予算が縮小されたため、ギャラを抑えられる彼にドラキュラ役のオファーがくる。たまたまベーラが舞台のツアーでロサンゼルスにいた

ハンガリー時代のルゴシ・ベーラ

ことも幸いした。1931年に封切されると、舞台で500回以上ドラキュラを演じてきたベーラの安定した演技は観客にも

批評家にも好評だった。映画は大ヒットとなり、早くも同年のうちに日本で上映されている。

　ドラキュラの地元と言える地で育ったこと、そして舞台から映画への移行期に活躍したことを思えば、ルゴシ・ベーラは、ブラム・ストーカーとヘンリー・アーヴィングの『ドラキュラ』を引き継ぎ、世界に広めた俳優だといえる。

　『ドラキュラ』が本格的にブームになりはじめるのは第二次世界大戦後の復興が一巡した1957年、本国イギリスで鬼才テレンス・フィッシャー監督が吸血鬼ものの2作目『吸血鬼ドラキュラ』(原題 *Horror of Dracula*) をリリースしてからである。主演はクリストファー・リー (1922-2015) で、ストーカーの原作を比較的忠実にたどっている。この作品を含め、ヴァン・ヘルシング役のピーター・カッシングと共演した3作は長ら

『吸血鬼ドラキュラ』 DVD 輸入盤

くドラキュラものの代名詞であった。リーはドラキュラものを7作撮り終えたあと、吸血鬼俳優となってしまうことを恐れて新境地アメリカに渡るが、1985年にはイギリスに帰国し、90才を超えるまでさまざまな役で俳優を続けた。

　1970年から1980年代はテレビ全盛のころで、制作会社ハマー・プロダクションはリーの吸血鬼映画の放映権を売りまくり、映画は世界中で繰り返し放映された。そのため長身で細面の彼が演じるドラキュラ像はもはや陳腐な印象を免れないが、それすなわち不動の定番である証左とも言えよう。

ヴァン・ヘルシングを演じる
カッシング

『ドラキュラ』 DVD 輸入盤

　その定番を破って高い評価を得たのが、フランシス・コッポラ監督の『ドラキュラ』(*Bram Stoker's Dracula*, 1992) である。ヴラド・ドラクルの存在も取り込んで、まさに映画の原題どおり、ブラム・ストーカーの世界の再解釈、再構築となっている。

　ひとりの女優ウィノナ・ライダーが、ミナ・ハーカーと、かつてヴラド・ドラクルが愛した妻の二役を演じることで、ドラキュラ伯爵の数百年の愛の渇望が基低音となり、副題 "Love Never Dies" が示唆するごとく恐怖よりむしろ「死を超える愛」がテーマとなる。音も絵も非常に濃厚で、セクシュアリティーが強調された迫力ある映像は、録音効果編集、メイクアップ、そして衣装デザインのアカデミー賞を受賞した。ゲイリー・オールドマン（映画『ハリー・ポッター』シリ

ウス役）演じるドラキュラの変幻する姿や、聖性と不潔さが合体するルーシーの死装束など、ことにコスチュームがすばらしい。これら衣装のデザインを担当したのは石岡瑛子 (1938-2012) で、かつて資生堂のアートディレクターなどを務めた日本人女性である。受賞後のインタヴューでは、「常に、コッポラ監督が想定し求めるイメージを大きく超えるような衣装の提案を心がけた」と述べている。ちなみに 2017 年、辻一弘が、映画『ウィンストン・チャーチル』の特殊メイク・ヘアで、主演のオールドマンと並んでアカデミー賞を受賞したことは記憶に新しいが、すでに彫刻家に転身していた辻を説得してメイクを引き受けさせたのはオールドマンだった。

参考文献：*Count Dracula Goes to the Movie: Stoker's Novel Adapted,* 3rd edition (Lyndon W. Joslin, McFarland Publishing, 2017)

Appendix

Chapter Introductions through Listening

Chapter 1

To the Borgo Pass

Solicitor, Jonathan Harker's diary written in Bistritz, Rumania

May 3rd

On the first of May, I left Munich for Transylvania. On the way, I was welcomed by [1   ] at the Golden Krone Hotel here in Bistritz. She asked me, "The English gentleman? Going to the Castle of Dracula in Transylvania?" When I said "Yes", [2   ].

Dear Friend,

Welcome to the Carpathians. Sleep well tonight. [3   ] Bukovina at three tomorrow. [4   ] at the Borgo Pass.

Your friend,
Count Dracula

Chapter 2

A prisoner of the Castle

Jonathan Harker's diary

May 7th

In the morning before dawn, I found a kind of library. Some of the shelves [1   ] England. Soon the Count came in and greeted me. "I learned your language through these books. I hope you can teach me [2   ]."

"But you speak English very well," I said.

"I am a noble here. But in London, I will be a stranger. I will be nobody there." He seemed to be concerned [3   ]. In fact, he sounded worried.

"May I come to the library when I want to?"

"Certainly. You may go anywhere you wish in this castle, [4   ]. We are in Transylvania. Transylvania is not England."

Chapter 3

In the vault

Jonathan Harker's diary

May 17th

The Count told me to write three letters; one saying, "[1
] in Transylvania and am leaving for London in a few days"; another saying, "[2]"; and the last one saying, "I have arrived at Bistritz."

I asked him [3]. He said "June 12th, June 19th, and June 29th respectively." Now I know [4].

Chapter 4

Lucy and her suitors

[1] *Miss Mina Murray and Miss Lucy Westenra*

May 9th

My dearest friend,

Forgive me, Lucy. [2].

Jonathan has written so little to me from Transylvania. But he is well and returns in a week.

[3] since we saw each other last time. I have heard [4].

Mina

Chapter 5

On the East Cliff

Mina Murray's diary

August 11th, 3 a.m.

I'm at Lucy's at her request. I'm glad to be with her but [1]. Lucy sleepwalked in her childhood for some time. Then she stopped. But she has started to sleepwalk again.

Earlier this evening, I suddenly woke up and I looked around in our bedroom. Her bed was empty. [2] in the house. And I noticed the front door was open. I ran to the West Cliff and looked across the harbour to the East Cliff where Lucy and I often go to spend time. I saw [3] on the bench we often sat on together. The person looked like Lucy. And then I saw a man bending over her. [4]

Chapter 6

The Professor researches

Dr Seward's diary

September 7th

When the transfusion was finished, Van Helsing said, "Now [1]." When Arthur kissed Lucy on her cheek, a narrow black band around her neck moved. Her fiancé did not see but Van Helsing and I noticed [2].

As soon as Arthur went down to take some port wine to warm his body, we examined the marks. There was [3]. Do these punctures have anything to do with her loss of blood? But if so, [4] on her pillow.

Chapter 7

Lucy passes away

Dr Seward's diary

September 19th

I received a telegram from Van Helsing only yesterday morning. He was worried because Lucy had to spend a night alone with her mother last night. We hurried to their house and [1]. But no one answered. We broke the lock and ran up to Lucy's bedroom. I cannot [2].

The two women were lying down on the bed. The old lady was covered with a white sheet. But Lucy was not. Her eyes were open and there was [3]. The garlic flowers were cast on the floor. The punctures on her throat were torn. They were [4]. The Professor bent over Lucy and listened to her heart. Then he cried out, "Brandy! Transfusion! Quick!"

Chapter 8

Setting Lucy free

Dr Seward's diary

September 29th

Van Helsing explained to Arthur and Quincy about "the undead". He also gave Arthur [1] Lucy in order to save her soul. Arthur was upset and furious at the beginning. We [2] we had collected about Lucy, including her memorandum. In the end, he understood.

When the four of us reached her tomb, the Professor asked me [3

] the previous night. I answered yes. Then we opened her coffin. [4   ].

Chapter 9

The confession of Renfield

Jonathan Harker's diary
October 1st, 5 a.m.

I [1   ] Mina at the asylum. I didn't [2
] this horrible business.

Quincy showed a silver whistle to us. "Carfax will be full of rats. If they appear, I will blow my whistle and my dogs will come." Then the Professor gave each of us a silver crucifix and a piece of sacred wafer.

Arriving at Carfax, we went straight into the underground chapel. There, everything was covered with dust. A terrible [3
]. "First, let us make sure how many boxes are here," said the Professor. There were only twenty-nine out of the fifty boxes [4
].

Chapter 10

Cornering the Count

Jonathan Harker's diary
October 3rd

[1   ] again. We decided to first sterilize the twenty-nine boxes placed in the chapel of Carfax before pursuing the Count to Piccadilly. The Professor said, "We have to be prepared for the most horrible and dangerous mission that each one of us has ever experienced. Here, [2
] that we will never give up and continue our fight till the monster perishes."

He then said to Mina, "You will be safe while we are out. I have put garlic flowers and crucifixes in your room [3   ]." Saying this, he touched her forehead with a piece of sacred wafer. She screamed. [4
] like a piece of hot metal.

Chapter 11

To Transylvania

Mina Harker's diary

October 5th, 5 p.m.

It was not difficult to find the ship that took the Count onto the route back to Transylvania, because there was only one ship going to Black Sea—the Czarina Catherine [1   ].

I'm going with the others this time. [2   ] when I am in the Count's territory. However, [3   ] where my husband had [4   ].

Chapter 12

The last battle

Mina Harker's diary

November 6th

Early in the evening, Professor Van Helsing and I started walking eastward to join Jonathan and the others. [1   ], we could move only slowly. But I knew [2   ] on the winding road. We looked back at the castle. It was standing on the high precipice [3   ]. The silhouette [4   ] was beautiful but terrifying.

使用した図版について

p.5 Bistritz in Hungary, Wikicommons

p.6 地図 Wikicommons, posted by Syria James

p.6 十字架の図　Pixabay

p.14 *The Vampire* by Sir Philip Burne-Jones, 1897, Wikicommons

p.16 *Dracula* Wordsworth Classics 1993 年版表紙

p.17 アーヴィング　John Irving, Wikicommons

p.17 ロンドン、ライシアム劇場　Lyceum Theatre, Wikicommons

p.17 ワイルド　Oscar Wilde, Wikicommons

p.18 ストーカー　Bram Stoker, Wikicommons

p.20 *Dracula* Riders and Sons 1916 年版表紙

p.24 *Dracula* wordsworth Classics 2012 年版表紙

p.27 Whitby Abbey, Wikicommons

p.28 地図 Pixabay

p.28 狼の写真 Pixabay

p.32 *Symphony in White No. 1* by J. M. Whistler, 1861-1862, Wikicommons

p.32 Whitby, the East Cliff, Pixabay

p.37 *Dracula* Silent Sundays Books 2013 年版表紙

p.38 バーンベリの肖像　Wikicommons

p.38 ヴラド 3 世肖像画 Wikicommons

p.38 オスマン帝国拡大の図 Pixabay

p.38 リュブリャナのシンボル、城壁のドラゴンの写真 Wikicommons

p.38 「串刺し王ヴラド 3 世」16 世紀の木版画 Wikicommons

p.39 John Irving as Shylock, Wikicommons

p.42 ニンニクの花の写真 Wikicommons

p.43 狼の写真 Pixabay

p.43 *Dracula* Marabout Fantastic Books 2009 年版表紙

p.48 *Dracula* Hammond Collection 1960 年版表紙

p.49 古い日記の図 Pixabay

p.50 夜の墓場の写真 Pixabay

p.50 イチイの木の写真　Wikicommons

p.53 *Dracula* Barnes & Noble Classics Series 表紙

p.55 Hrabka Tomb, created and posted by Rama, Wikicommons

p.56 古いタイプライターの図 Pixabay

p.61 銀の笛の図 Pixabay

p.61 ドブネズミの図 "Stuff in the basement" posted by J.C. Schaap, Pixabay

p.61 19 世紀のピカデリー・サーカス Piccadilly Circus in 1896, Wikicommons

p.65 *Dracula* BBC Audio Book 2001 パッケージ

p.66 『ロビンソン・クルーソー』初版扉 Wikicommons

p.66 ウォルポールの屋敷内部 Strawberry Hill Library, Wikicommons

p.67「血まみれの尼僧」の挿絵 *Agness*, Wikicommons

p.67『吸血鬼バーニー』表紙 *Varney the Vampire, Feast of Blood* Wikicommons

p.67『吸血鬼カーミラ』*Carmilla*43 Amazon e-book, 2017

p.72 鍵束の図 Pixabay

p.72 札束の図 Pixabay

p.77 The old route of the Oriental Express, posted by Historicroute, Pixabay

p.77 蒸気機関車の図 Pixabay

p.78 断崖の城の図（部分）posted by Darksouls, Pixabay

p.79 森の城壁の図（部分）posted by Darksouls, Pixabay

p.81 棺台と棺の図（部分）Pixabay

p.83 *Dracula* Penguin Books 2001 年版表紙

p.83 古い双眼鏡の図 Pixabay

p.84 ライフル銃の図 Winchester rifle, Pixabay

p.84 カルパチア山脈の日没 The Carpathians, Pixabay

p.85 城 の 廃 墟 の 図 A ruined castle, created and posted by Franciszek Vetulan, Wikicommons

p.88 廃墟の図（部分）Pixabay

p.89 *Dracula* Universal Pictures 1931 年作品復刻版 DVD パッケージ

p.89 ハンガリー時代のルゴシ・ベーラ　FOTO:FORTEPAN /adományozó SALY NOÉMI Lugosi Bela, Wikicommons

p.90『吸血鬼ドラキュラ』*Horror of Dracula* Hammer Film Production 1957 年作品復刻版 DVD パッケージ

p.90 ヴ ァ ン ・ ヘ ル シ ン グ を 演 じ る カ ッ シ ン グ Peter Cushing as Van Helsing, Wikicommons

p.90『ドラキュラ』*Bram Stoker's Dracula* Columbia Pictures 1992 年作品 DVD パッケージ

上記以外の図（スティール含む）はすべて Dracula Universal Pictures 1931 年作品から。

音声ファイルのダウンロード方法

英宝社ホームページ（http://www.eihosha.co.jp/）の
「テキスト音声ダウンロード」バナーをクリックすると、
音声ファイルダウンロードページにアクセスできます。

Dracula in simple English (retold)

ドラキュラ リトールド版

2019 年 1 月 15 日　初　版　　　　2021 年 3 月 31 日　初版第二刷

著　者　細　川　祐　子

発　行　者　佐　々　木　　元

発　行　所　株式会社　英　宝　社
〒101-0032 東京都千代田区岩本町 2-7-7
TEL 03 (5833) 5870-1 FAX 03 (5833) 5872

[製版・表紙デザイン：伊谷企画／印刷・製本：日本ハイコム株式会社]

ISBN 978-4-269-01432-9 C1082